ELLIOT

MISSIONARY MARTYR

SUSAN MARTINS MILLER

BARBOUR
PUBLISHING

Jim
ELLIOT

ISBN 1-59310-382-4

Cover illustration © Dick Bobnick
Cover design by Douglas Miller (mhpubarts.com)

Published by Barbour Publishing, Inc., P.O. Box 719, Uhrichsville, Ohio 44683, www.barbourbooks.com

Our mission is to publish and distribute inspirational products offering exceptional value and biblical encouragement to the masses.

ecpa Member of the
Evangelical Christian
Publishers Association

Printed in the United States of America.
5 4 3 2

INTRODUCTION

W hat does God want me to do?
    The people of God have been asking this question for thousands of years.

For a few, the answer comes quickly and clearly, and they respond with a certainty of conviction that befuddles friends and family. For many others, God's leading is a bit foggy, if not downright obscure at times. This is why "How to Know the Will of God" is a topic that draws an eager crowd whenever a seminar or class is offered. But can it really be reduced to a step-by-step process?

We can ponder the question philsophically and reason that what God wants most from us is a commitment to live lives that demonstrate His love and draw other people to Him. As long as what we do does not contradict the truth God has revealed in the Bible, whatever decisions we make will please God. We can choose freely where to go to school, whom to marry, what career to pursue, where to live, and so forth. Admittedly, in certain instances we may have a sense of specific leading toward a particular decision. When that happens, we should follow that leading. But that does not always happen, so in general, we can please and serve God in whatever decisions we make.

We can also stand at the other end of the spectrum and argue that God has a specific plan for each one of us. At every decision point, we should find out God's will in that circumstance and do it. Whom to marry, where to work, when to change jobs or begin a new ministry—God has a specific answer to every question. And His answer may not be the most obvious or easy choice. We must be careful to find God's will objectively and not be influenced by circumstances, pressing needs, or emotion. It is better to do nothing than to take action without being sure of God's leading.

This theological diversity may not be the only factor that influences how we respond to the question, "What does God want me to do?" Personality enters in. God did not create us all alike. Neither does the redemptive process make us all alike. Even when united by a desire to serve God, we remain different from each other, with individual differences and abilities. Some people leap at the chance to do something daring, while others cautiously stick to the sensible. Some move from one thing to another as their interests change, while others dedicate decades to a single purpose. Some respond wholeheartedly to the stimulation of life and people around them, while others keep aloof, afraid of compromising their beliefs somehow. Some make up their own minds, while others are influenced by persuasive talk. These differences do not diminish the common motive to do what God wants us to do.

God is not limited by our personalities—He created them. Neither is He limited by theological inclinations—He can change those. No matter where we stand individually on the continuums of theology and personality, God's people want to listen to His voice.

The story of Jim Elliot's brief adult life is an account of how he heard and responded to God's voice. Though not all will agree with his interpretations, his story is an exploration of one person's understanding of the will of God. Most likely his personality affected his interpretations as much as his theology did. This resulted in an amazing singleness of purpose for his own life. In addition, because he was not hesitant to act publicly on his convictions, his singleness of purpose swept up several other people and their families.

Onlookers five decades after his death may speculate about how Jim's life—and the lives of others he worked with—might have been different if he had made other decisions at key turning points. Would other decisions have been right, wrong, or simply different?

Following the will of God is not a fool-proof process. Even missionaries like Jim Elliot are human and fallible. But no matter what our choices, and no matter what motivates them, God is powerful enough to bring good where His children can see none.

THE LIFE OF JIM ELLIOT

October 1927	Jim Elliot is born in Oregon
September 1945	Jim enters Wheaton College in Wheaton, Illinois
December 1946	Jim attends an InterVarsity mission conference in Toronto, Canada
Summer 1947	Jim goes on a mission trip to Mexico and begins to focus interest on Latin America
December 1947	Jim spends Christmas holidays with the Howard family in New Jersery
May 1948	Jim and Elisabeth realize they love each other
June 1948	Elisabeth graduates from college
September 1948	Jim and Elisabeth visit each other in Wheaton
October 1948	Jim and Elisabeth begin corresponding
December 1948	Jim attends second InterVarsity mission conference in Urbana, Illinois
Spring 1949	Jim undergoes a "renaissance" and challenges Ed McCully to be a missionary
June 1949	Jim graduates from Wheaton and returns to Portland, Oregon
September 1949	Elisabeth visits the Elliot family in Portland
Summer 1950	Jim attends linguistic training in Oklahoma; David Howard gets married; Jim commits to going to Ecuador
Fall 1950	Ed McCully decides to leave law school and consider missionary work

January 1951	Jim begins ministry in Chester, Illinois, with Ed
June 1951	Ed marries Marilou, and Bill Cathers marries Irene; Jim returns to Oregon
February 1952	Jim and Pete Fleming arrive in Ecuador
April 1952	Elisabeth arrives in Ecuador
August 1952	Jim and Pete finish language study and go to the Shandia mission station
December 1952	Ed and Marilou McCully arrive in Ecuador
February 1953	First Quichua Bible Conference
July 1953	Flood at Shandia destroys a year's work
October 1953	Jim and Elisabeth get married in Quito and move to Puyupungu to establish a new station
February 1954	Second Quichua Bible Conference
June 1954	Jim and Elisabeth move to Shandia
February 1955	Jim and Elisabeth's daughter, Valerie, is born at Shell Mera
September 1955	Nate Saint and Ed McCully see Auca villages for the first time
October 1955	Search for Aucas begins in earnest; first gift drop is made
December 1955	Plans are finalized for ground contact with Aucas
January 3, 1956	The missionaries land on Palm Beach and set up camp
January 6, 1956	George, Delilah, and another Auca woman come to the beach
January 8, 1956	Last radio contact with Marj Saint at Shell Mera

SOUTH AMERICA

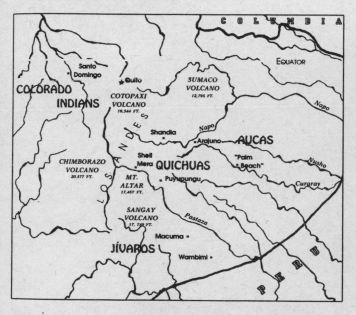

Ecuador, Spanish for equator, contains a wide variety of climates. Over half—three-fourths in the 1950s—of the country is covered with the dense green of tropical rain forests. The mighty Andes Mountain range divides east from west and boasts approximately thirty volcanoes.

The Eastern Lowlands, the land of the Quichuas, Jívaros, and Aucas, extend from the eastern slopes of the Andes to the border with Peru. The region is lined with many rivers that eventually connect with the Amazon River in Brazil.

ONE

George peered up at the object in the air, puzzled, curious. Why did it not fall from the sky? The birds made no sound when they flew, but this bright yellow mystery roared as it broke from the ground and burst onto the horizon. On the ground, its sound made George want to cover his ears. When it was aloft and gliding like the birds, while he stood on the beach, the sound was only a buzz.

Delilah watched George's movements with reluctant interest. She had come to the beach knowing that George intended to give her away, either as a gift or as a trade for some of the curiosities the strangers possessed. Delilah and another woman, perhaps twice as old as Delilah, stood on the riverbank while George called out to the strangers on the other side. Five of them gaped over the water and rushed around like nervous chickens. No matter why she had come, Delilah was curious now. The strangers were saying something in response to George's greeting, but it was difficult to be sure what it was. She listened more intently. Finally, the sound formed in her ears. *Puinani! Welcome!* They spoke her language, but it sounded unfamiliar; they needed practice.

One of the strangers took off the cloths that draped his body. *Why would anyone wear so much cloth?* Delilah wondered; she herself, like the rest of her people, wore only a string of beads around her waist. With his skin exposed, he waded into the river. Surely he wanted to be friends. Perhaps Delilah would be given to him. His companions seemed anxious and called to him with words Delilah did not understand, and for a moment, he stopped and looked back. But he continued his slow journey. Delilah looked from the stranger to George to the other woman. George was not moving. Why not? Had they not come this far in order to see the strangers close up? Why should they wait? Delilah inched forward and stepped off a log. The stranger was very near now, sloshing toward her with his hand outstretched. Feeling very brave, she took his hand—how pale it was—and followed him back across the river.

Once ashore again, Delilah was free to investigate the real reason for her curiosity, the strange object for which she had no word. She rubbed herself against it, wondering what it was made of, then stretched her arms out to her sides to playfully swoop as she had seen it do.

George was soon beside her, examining it as well. But he had not come across the river just to look and touch. He told the strangers he wanted to ride in the air as he had seen them do, but they did not answer. Instead, they turned to each other and spoke those strange sounds again. Why did they speak words of welcome and then not respond to his words? Like Delilah, George gestured and raised his eyes to the sky. Now they understood his wish. Then he put his machete and a gift of valuable items on the sitting place. He was ready to go.

One of the strangers sat next to George with his hands on some sticks and circles. They soon swept up into the air, and George grinned. This is what he had come for. The stranger knew how to make the great bird fly; George paid no attention to that but instead leaned out an opening in the wall next to him to see where he had come from. He saw his village and his eyes widened. He yelled and waved to his people, chuckling at their surprised faces when they recognized him. Who else in his tribe could claim such an experience?

On the ground again, the stranger and his friends stuck sticks in the sand and pulled out a small, silent version of the mysterious and powerful bird that was not really a bird. This small one had no strength of its own and smashed into the sticks in the sand. But then the strangers took away the sticks, smoothed the sand, and brought in the small bird again. This time they set it down softly in the sand. George looked around the beach and understood. They could put down the great object alongside the river because there were no trees. But his village was surrounded by a forest that had grown for thousands of years. He had seen his village from the sky, but these strangers could never go there unless he took down some trees and made a soft spot, like the beach.

On Sunday morning, Pete climbed into the Piper Cub and said good-bye to his wife and the others seeing him off. "I believe today's the day," he said.

After setting up camp with three other missionaries several days ago, Pete and his companion, Nate, had been flying over the beach and the village, dropping small gifts—ribbons, machetes, knives, clothing. Actually, the missionaries had begun dropping gifts into jungle clearings long before they had landed the plane on the beach. For three months they had worked toward this day. And now, at last, they had had their first visitors from the jungle. On the beach, they stretched rubber bands, inflated balloons, and masterfully snapped yo-yos up and down a string. The tribesmen who had come to the beach were enchanted by these strange things. But this had been only a handful of the Auca tribe, whose village lay deep within the jungle where a plane could not land—and to which the American missionaries had not been invited. Finally, they produced a photograph of a young woman who had left the tribe, hoping that the villagers would recognize her and receive the outsiders as friends on her behalf.

Nate and Pete had flown over the village that morning, trying to signal to the Aucas that the missionaries were by the river. On the first flight, Nate had called out, "Come, come, come!" in their own language and had thrown down a blanket and a pair of shorts as a gesture of friendship.

On the second flight over the village, George had appeared. Pete and Nate, and their coworkers Jim, Ed, and Roger, were encouraged by the progress. Their excitement swelled as they contemplated reaching a tribe deep within Ecuador, a people who had never seen a church, never read a book, never sung a hymn, never heard a missionary preach.

After George and the women appeared, the missionaries hoped that more representatives of the tribe would come. Hour after hour they waited on the beach, grasping at activities to keep themselves from complete idleness. Finally, Nate made a solo flight, surveying the village once more. This time he saw only a handful of women and children. Where were the men? A moment later, he had his answer. He saw them moving as a group toward the beach. Swiftly, he turned the plane around and returned to the beach, shouting, "This is it, guys! They're on the way!"

Nate got on the radio to communicate with his wife. It was twelve-thirty. The men were approaching. Nate promised to radio again at four-thirty.

Standing on the beach waiting for the contingent he knew was coming, Jim Elliot had no regrets about having been the first to wade into the water to greet George and Delilah a couple of days earlier. He knew that years of patient preparation were about to be rewarded. He had waited a long time for this day.

Jim Elliot, born October 8, 1927, grew up on the slopes of Mt. Tabor in western Oregon. His mother, Clara, was a chiropractor, and his father, Fred, was a Bible teacher and evangelist for a group of Christians commonly known as Plymouth Brethren. When the Brethren gathered, they called themselves assemblies, rather than churches. Fred Elliot read the Bible to his children every day and prayed *with* them as well as *for* them. The children went to worship meetings from the time they were babies. Their mother held strong views about many things, including the firm belief that it was good for children to sit through an adult meeting.

The intensity of the Plymouth Brethren bore fruit in Jim's development. From early childhood, Jim learned a single-mindedness and seriousness about spiritual things.

Jim was six when he told his mother that the Lord Jesus could come and take the whole family. Even at that young age, he was sure that he was saved; but his younger sister was too young to understand about Jesus yet.

The Elliots wanted the best for their children, and although the family enjoyed the beauty of their surroundings, they did not take things for granted. Giving their children the best did not mean conforming to the trends around them. For instance, Clara Elliot did not believe in buying pasteurized milk for her family; she stuck to what she knew was good for her children. When the children needed disciplining, Fred and Clara emphasized obedience and honesty—basic traits that formed the foundation for spiritual development as well as family relationships. Growing up in this atmosphere, Jim was accustomed to good hard work, whether physical or mental. In fact, a childhood friend who visited after school one day was impressed by the number of chores Jim had to do. Even more striking, though, was Jim's careful, methodical approach to feeding the chickens, stoking the furnace, tidying up the yard, and running errands. Even as a child, Jim was systematic and strategic in his activities.

All this seriousness did not mean that Jim was unable to have fun. During his grade school and teen years, he was particularly close to two other boys who were his companions on hunting and camping expeditions. In fact, it was Jim who instigated the camping trips. He persuaded his friends to visit the local thrift shops to assemble their gear, then the three of them set out hitchhiking. On their first outing, they managed to shoot a pet duck along the edge of a golf course. Of course, when they realized what they had done, they asked God to comfort the duck's owner in her sorrow!

Jim played high school football and participated in theatrical productions. His teachers even urged him to consider a career in the professional theater. He was handsome, engaging, intelligent, and genuinely talented. No doubt he could succeed even in a difficult profession like acting. But Jim had other things on his mind. While the theater was an interesting diversion, it did not hold an ultimate purpose for him.

A friend found him running the track near the school one day, straining and sweating against the rigorous pace he had set. When asked why he was doing this, Jim responded, "Bodily exercise is profitable for a little." His mind was fixed beyond the immediacy of teenage attractions on the future, to a time when God might ask more of him. Jim wanted to be ready to give it, physically and spiritually.

This meant Jim was wary of anything that might distract him from God's unfolding purpose for his life—and a major distraction was the opposite sex. Even as a teenager, Jim was dubious about women. While friendships with other boys thrived, he intentionally withdrew from being friends with girls. "Domesticated males aren't much use for adventure," he said. Whenever he observed that a young woman caught the eye of his friend at a social gathering, Jim would maneuver over to his friend and softly say, "Beware, Fisher, beware." [1]

At an age when most young people are self-conscious and sensitive about not fitting in with their peers, Jim forged his way independently and confidently. Perhaps the non-conformist background of the Plymouth Brethren was bred into him so that it became his outlook as well. As a teenager, he carried a Bible along with his textbooks and spoke freely about what it contained. He did not care if people saw him praying before he ate his lunch. He publicly refused to buy tickets to a school dance because of his personal belief that Christians should not dance. As a member of the public speaking club, he was assigned to make a political speech during a presidential campaign and refused—risking expulsion from the club—on the grounds that a follower of Jesus could not participate in war or politics.

The Elliot family was not wealthy, but this fact did not concern Jim. He had learned well that God would provide. Uncertain where his ongoing support would come from, he set off for Wheaton College in Wheaton, Illinois, in the fall of 1945. He was on his own now. No longer a child taking cues from his parents, he was a young man who would put to the test all that had been formed in him to that point.

TWO

Is it so bad for a student to begin college unsure of a future profession? After all, in college, students are exposed to things they have never experienced before. They try their hand at new skills and challenging disciplines and discover their God-given gifts in the process.

This was not the case, however, for Jim Elliot. Unlike many college freshmen, Jim Elliot knew what he wanted when he entered Wheaton College. His nurturing, expressive, and spiritually vibrant upbringing had brought him to the point where he began his higher education with the goal of becoming an overseas missionary. His intent was to be prepared for any challenge he might face in following this calling. And it was a calling. Still, it is not unusual for a young adult's sense of call to change as it matures, perhaps taking on a whole new form. The most genuine of calls might be revealed a step at a time. Would this be the experience of Jim Elliot?

While Jim had no idea about the country to which he would go, he was fixed from the start on going anywhere God might send him. He made no secret of this on Wheaton's campus. He soon gained a reputation for having a one-track mind. His friends were those who were also planning to be missionaries. His activities were those that would prepare him to be a missionary. As engaging and friendly as Jim was, he still chose to stay behind certain fences. No doubt some of his peers saw his single-mindedness as an eccentricity to which they could not relate.

Jim took college seriously. He looked on the college years as years of preparation to be ready for the Lord's plan. This attitude called for discipline in every aspect of his life. Many students enter college unsure of what they will study or what career they will pursue. Many also consider the social aspects of college life to be important in developing into a well-rounded person with mature skills in relating to other people and in solving problems. Academic success is not the complete process. To Jim, these other dimensions of college life were dubious, if not entirely frivolous. He guarded against distraction with discipline and focus. While other students pursued a multitude of choices in their activities, Jim Elliot limited himself to those activities that he thought directly related to his purpose of getting ready to serve God. He had to remain clear-headed, focused, and keep his eyes on his goal.

Developing his spirituality was of utmost importance. Perhaps naively, Jim assumed that other students were on the same track, despite their indulgence in activities that appeared to him unspiritual. Lacking inhibitions, he would wave to a friend across the campus and shout, "Glory, brother, what's your verse for the day?" The implication, of course, was that the friend should have had daily devotions, during which time God would surely have revealed a verse for the day. Jim was particularly likely to raise this question at mealtime in the dining hall, assuming that his companions had disciplined themselves with morning devotions.

Some fellow students began to avoid sitting with him at meals for fear that he would ask their verses for the day. With few words, Jim could make a student feel that he or she had already failed the Lord for that day because of an inability to answer that simple question. Whether it was his well-meaning intention to remind his fellow students about the importance of spiritual discipline, or whether he was genuinely oblivious to the fact that his questions made his friends squirm, who can say? In any event, his reputation formed early in his college career.

Jim was not well known on campus during his freshman year, largely because he did not live at the college. Rather, he lived in a nearby community with an aunt and uncle. Outside the classroom, his interaction with other students was limited. This did not bother Jim, because he had not come to college to cavort with the student body. He never fully understood the mentality of students who pursued diversions beyond academic requirements and spiritual development.

Everything Jim did during that first year of college had a specific purpose—to make him ready for the future. When he ate lunch in the school's dining hall, he chose his food carefully, eating fresh fruits, vegetables, and limited starches or desserts. This was the diet followed by the wrestling team, of which Jim was a member. Although he had not wrestled in high school, he easily qualified for Wheaton's varsity wrestling team during his freshman year.

Wheaton College was a small school, but few other comparable schools had wrestling teams. Because of this, the Wheaton wrestlers competed with athletes from large, intimidating universities. The first college wrestling meet Jim participated in was held at the University of Illinois at Urbana, Illinois. It so happened that the University of Illinois had a very good team that year, competing at championship levels. Jim's first match was against the national champion for his weight class.

Although he had qualified for the team, Jim was a beginning wrestler. He lacked formal coaching, and he knew very little about technique. His competitor quickly put an experienced hold on Jim. Jim wriggled out of it. A few seconds later, the university wrestler put another hold on him. Again Jim wriggled out of it.

Over and over again this happened. Before long, the national champion was swearing under his breath before attempting yet another hold on the novice Jim Elliot. He was never able to pin Jim down. This was the day Jim's teammates discovered he was double-jointed. They dubbed him "Rubberneck Elliot."

Was Jim enjoying wrestling? It must have been fun to frustrate the national champion. But this was secondary to Jim. He was not wrestling because he liked wrestling, but because wrestling was a means of keeping his body fit and healthy and strong enough for missionary work. He qualified for the varsity team, but beyond that he was not an outstanding wrestler.

To Jim, it did not matter whether he won or lost; he wrestled because of the discipline and physical fitness it required—characteristics that had direct relevance to his life goals. Any pleasure the activity may have brought him or anyone else was strictly an extra benefit.

Jim's spiritual perseverance paid off. Near the end of his first year of college, Jim wrote to his family that it had been a profitable year because he had drawn closer to God and discovered truths in the Bible. He was glad to see that Christianity was more than a padded pew or a dim cathedral. It was a real, living, daily experience. [1]

Jim had not seen his family during the school year. With summer looming, he set out for home. Economics meant that hitchhiking was the route home from Wheaton, near Chicago, across the continent to Portland, Oregon. Jim wrangled a total of twenty rides in seventy hours, never waiting more than fifteen minutes for a ride. He arrived home with $1.32 in his pocket, all the while praising the Lord for providing what he had needed. After spending a quiet summer with his family, he returned to Wheaton in the fall of 1946.

During his sophomore year of college, Jim lived closer to campus and was more involved with activities. He became treasurer of the sophomore class. A wrestling teammate, David Howard, was class president, and the two of them worked together as class officers, strengthening a friendship that had begun on the wrestling team. However, Jim did wonder whether he ought to be serving as a class officer; was it promoting spirituality, either for himself or his classmates? The activities were difficult to justify in his mind, particularly because of some of the shenanigans that fell to class officers to oversee.

In 1946 Wheaton College still maintained the tradition of the sophomores hazing the freshman class. As class president, Dave Howard was responsible to organize the crazy pranks that the freshmen were required to perform under the direction of the sophomores. But he needed help, and he turned to his friends.

Dave recruited Jim to serve as chief judge of the sophomore court. If a freshman was ruled guilty of a violation of the regulations which the sophomores had placed on the freshmen, he or she would be given a ticket and have to appear in sophomore court. Their punishment would be meted out as the judge saw fit. Tickets were dispensed for such things as not wearing the freshman dink (a little cap), or not dressing in the costume prescribed for the day.

Punishment for these crimes consisted of whacks on the backside or other mild chastisement. Although it was contrary to his usual pietistic outlook, Jim agreed to serve as chief judge in the sophomore court and dutifully dispensed sentences for offending freshmen. Later, though, he felt guilty—probably for a breach in his own spirituality more than for any harm done in the name of fun.

Jim toyed with other student activities that fall in what seemed to be a well-meaning attempt to enter the mainstream of student life. He went to a football game that fall for the first time with mixed feelings. Although he had played football in high school, he now questioned the value of a spectator activity that consisted largely of sitting in the bleachers and shouting. There did not seem to be much point in it. After all, it was not as if the crowd was shouting praise to God. It was just a silly competition. He returned to his room more convinced than ever that his time was better spent alone in fellowship with God. [2]

Even Jim's academic pursuits came second to his spiritual development. At the end of the first semester of his sophomore year, he had to admit to his parents that his grades were, as he expected, lower than the previous semester. But he made no apology. He knew he had let his academic studies suffer in favor of studying the Bible more. In his mind, he was not working toward a B.A. but a degree of A.U.G., "approved unto God."[3]

Though he had little use for football or basketball games, Jim was nevertheless interested in connecting with fellow students—but on a different plane. He sought out others who shared his interest in foreign missions and participated in activities organized by that group. Jim was involved in the activities of the Student Foreign Missions Fellowship.

In the spring semester of his sophomore year, teams of six students made visits to student groups affiliated with InterVarsity on various campuses in the area. One of the Wheaton students would be a song leader, and the other five would speak for about ten minutes each, covering the need for missionaries and modern methods for missions, as well as the practical aspects of physical labor and health precautions. Jim's topic that spring was the Holy Spirit in missions, and he spoke vigorously about it.

This experience was one of the pieces in the puzzle Jim was gradually solving. His first two years of college had been significant largely because it had been during this time that he had come face to face with the command of Jesus Christ to go into the world and preach the gospel.

During this time he gathered statistics about missions and copied them carefully into a small black notebook that he carried with him for years. He learned that:

- 1,700 languages did not have a word of the Bible translated.
- 90 percent of the people who volunteer for the mission field never got there.
- 64 percent of the world had never heard of Christ.
- 5,000 people died every hour.
- There was one Christian worker for every 50,000 people in foreign lands, while there was one to every 500 in the United States.[4]

The impact of this information was staggering to Jim. How could he possibly consider remaining in the United States in the face of this reality? He was an intelligent young man, physically fit, who could have chosen to pursue any career he wanted. But he was convinced that justifying a life in the States was too great a task; he was headed to the foreign mission field.

Before going home for a visit with his family that summer, Jim hitchhiked to Mexico with a college friend whose parents were missionaries there. He spent six weeks in Mexico, soaking up the language and principles of mission work. By the end of six weeks, he felt he was ready to attempt a talk to a group of 150 children.

To everyone's surprise, he decided to give the talk in Spanish without translation. When he lacked vocabulary, he would draw a picture until someone gave him the words he needed—usually one of the children. Though it was far from perfect, he persisted and completed his first foreign presentation of the gospel.

Jim hitchhiked back to Oregon, confident that God was calling him to Latin America.

THREE

Staying in school takes money—lots of it. Parents sacrifice and go into debt to keep their children in college. Even so, money may run out. Jim Elliot did not expect to complete more than two years at Wheaton. But when money was available for him to continue in the fall of 1947, he took this as a sign from God that he should return to Wheaton to complete his degree. He decided to major in Greek for two reasons. First, he wanted to be able to understand the original language of the New Testament for his own spiritual growth. Secondly, he believed that knowing Greek would help him translate the Bible into a primitive language at some point in the future. No other major would prepare him for his future missionary work in quite the same way. While other majors might have indirect benefits, every hour spent studying Greek would put him closer to translating the Bible into another language.

Jim and Dave Howard now lived across the hall from each other in the newest dormitory on campus. The dorm was for freshmen, and as upperclassmen, Jim and Dave were dorm counselors. They each roomed with a freshman, but they spent so much time together, they developed a relationship more characteristic of roommates than neighbors across the hall.

Jim concentrated on his academic work and his Bible study. During his first two years of college, he had earned the reputation of being a woman-hater. In his devotion to spiritual development, he had eliminated from his schedule any activities that he considered frivolous or unnecessary. Dating was among those non-essentials, quite close to the top of the list. Nothing that might distract him from his pursuit of the will of God had any place in his life. This was particularly frustrating to the young women at Wheaton, since Jim was attractive, athletic, and smart—a prime catch if anyone could catch him. But he seemed to have no interest in women and did not go out of his way to befriend them. In fact, he went out of his way to avoid them. He stuck to his homework and his Bible study.

Dave, however, was cultivating a romantic interest that year. "I specifically remember coming back one night from a basketball game," Dave recalls. "Jim was studying the Bible in his room. He was still in a stage where going to a basketball or a football game or a class party was second-class Christianity. It was a waste of time that you could have been spending in prayer and Bible study. I came into the room and Jim looked up from his Bible out of the corner of his eye, and in a very suspicious way said, 'Have you been out with Phyllis again?' When I confessed that I had been, he simply sighed and turned back to his Bible study, giving me the silent treatment. The implication was obvious. I had been wasting an evening, while he had been redeeming the time by studying the Bible."

Then Jim met Elisabeth.

A fellow Greek major, Elisabeth Howard had an almost identical class schedule during Jim's junior year, which was her senior year. She eyed Jim across the aisle of their ancient history class: just under six feet tall, gray-blue eyes that looked blue with the sky-colored sweater he often wore with gray flannel pants, matching socks, and bow ties. After a while, she realized that this was her brother's buddy from the wrestling squad. She had heard Dave talk about Jim. In fact, Dave had suggested that she might enjoy meeting Jim, but Elisabeth had taken little notice. Now, however, her perspective was changing.

Jim was changing, too. He began staying a few minutes after class to chat with Elisabeth. Having identical classes gave them a good starting point to break down conversational barriers. From there they moved on to more personal topics. One day in October 1947, Jim impulsively asked Elisabeth for a date. She accepted but later broke the date—and suffered recriminations from her female classmates for having passed up such an unheard-of opportunity as a date with Jim Elliot.

Not knowing that Jim and his sister had struck up this friendship, and knowing that Jim would not be able to go home to Portland for Christmas, Dave Howard generously and innocently invited Jim to spend the holidays with the Howard family in New Jersey. The Howards were delighted with Jim, who flashed his smile and brightened up the staid New England household. He fixed what needed fixing, wiped dishes voluntarily, sledded and skated with David and Elisabeth's younger siblings, and shoveled snow. He was generally helpful to everyone in the family.

What he did for Elisabeth, though, was to keep her up late at night, when the rest of the family had gone to bed, discussing everything from war to the role of women in the church. Most of the time, Elisabeth disagreed with his opinions, but clearly she found him interesting. Still, their budding relationship was restrained and discreet. Even David, who lived across the hall from Jim, was unaware of the depths it reached in the months between Christmas and the spring.

Jim's relationship with Elisabeth was no overnight turnaround. He had not suddenly decided to abandon the principles that had guided him up to this point. Dating was still not a priority in his life. Yet he could not deny his affection and attraction to Elisabeth. He struggled ferociously with the implications of this friendship. He had set his sights on a single life for so long—one dedicated only to serving God—that he hardly knew what to make of his surfacing emotions.

Shortly after the Christmas spent with the Howard family, Jim began a diary. And, of course, the diary had a purpose. Writing about his experiences and relationships like many people do was not Jim's approach. He used his diary as a place to record his insights into the Bible, with sentence prayers that applied those truths to his life. After the intense holiday season with Elisabeth, Jim might have also used the diary as a place to make sense of his emotions. But he did not. He stuck to his more spiritual purposes. Whatever his feelings for Elisabeth were at that point in time, they did not penetrate his journal.

One of the first entries, made January 29, 1949, says: "God, I pray, light these idle sticks of my life and may I burn up for Thee. Consecrate my life, my God, for it is Thine. I seek not a long life but a full one like Yours, Lord Jesus." [1]

As his writing habit matured, he reflected also on his personal experiences. In April of that year, he wrote: "Yesterday Ruth Stam (a fellow student) said to me that someone had made this statement about my manner: 'We know he is humble, but we wish he would act it.' How they can be so certain of the first statement I don't know; my own proud heart is fully aware now of its self-exaltation. Probably I have been a hypocrite clever enough to conceal what really lies there. But the last clause speaks to my heart in powerful tones. Often I have felt this self-exertion coming out and know now that my mode of self-expression must have been, yea, and is, most offensive. I cannot do anything about this, Father. I've tried again and again to be silent and act gravely and soberly as I feel a holy man ought, but to little avail. Either someone asks if I'm sick or my own affable, self-confident nature bubbles over with something that breaks the spell." [2]

Two days later he wrote: "Father, take my life, even my blood, if Thou wilt, and consume it with Thine enveloping fire. I would not save it, for it is not mine to save. Have it, Lord, have it all. Pour out my life as an oblation for the world. Blood is only of value as it flows before Thine altars."[3]

During the months between Christmas and spring, Jim's journal entries gave no hint of his relationship with Elisabeth Howard. His thoughts, at least for purposes of his journal, focused on single-mindedly offering himself to God's service and agonizing over his spiritual readiness for the tasks ahead of him as a missionary in South America. Perhaps avoiding an encounter with his conflicting emotions in his journal was an attempt to keep his feelings separated and under control. His journal from those months displays a spiritual function focused on putting himself through his paces and making sure he was fit to serve God.

That he did not write about Elisabeth in these months is as significant as what he might have written. The first volume of his journal reads like an extended Bible study. Only months later did he dare to put down on paper his feelings for Elisabeth—when they reached a proportion from which he could no longer turn away. Despite the omission from his journal, the relationship between Jim and Elisabeth raced forward.

However, Jim and Elisabeth did not have a typical dating relationship. Their one and only date, in April of 1948, was to attend a missionary meeting at Moody Church in Chicago. No doubt, to many of their classmates, such a spiritual context would not even have constituted a date. But it was typical of the tone of their relationship. They also sat together in Greek classes and often studied their assignments together; these encounters also led to other opportunities to be together.

Jim organized an evangelistic trip to Indiana and handpicked the fellow Wheaton students who would accompany him, including Elisabeth. As they drove through the night, she stayed awake to keep Jim company. While the others slept, Jim and Elisabeth took advantage of the chance for long, satisfying conversation. This was not a traditional date, but it certainly contributed to the growth of their relationship.

Their relationship was not without bumps along the way. One night, Jim phoned Elisabeth's dorm and invited her to the student recreation center for a Coke. She raced right over, never expecting what Jim had in mind. He rebuked her as a "sister in Christ" for her reticence. He thought she should allow Christ to make her more open and friendly. [4]

For many college couples, such a rebuke would have been the end of the romance. Elisabeth was hurt by Jim's words, yes, but she appreciated his ability to speak in a straightforward way. In the end, it increased her attraction to him.

During that semester, Elisabeth joined a group of students who rode the train to Chicago to talk about Jesus with people in railway stations. To her amazement, she discovered that Jim was a part of the group. One Saturday night, coming back to Wheaton, Jim dropped into the seat next to Elisabeth to indulge in conversation about their experiences. [5] This sort of conversation was confirmation that their minds were on the same track.

Such was the nature of their courtship, if it could be called that.

On Memorial Day of 1948, Jim and Elisabeth attended a picnic sponsored by the missions fellowship in which they were both active. Afterwards, they were among those who lingered to clean up, discreetly keeping their distance and attending to separate tasks. Then

Jim asked to walk Elisabeth home. They started their walk in silence, which Jim quickly broke. He stunned Elisabeth by announcing that they needed to clear up how they felt about each other. Although Elisabeth had tried to disguise the extent of her interest in Jim, he was intuitively aware of her growing feelings.

Instead of walking back to the campus, they turned around and went back to the picnic site where they were now alone. They spent seven hours drenched in conversation about what their relationship meant or did not mean.[6]

Jim told Elisabeth that he loved her—but quickly added that he had no sign from God that he was to marry her, or anyone else for that matter. Until that moment of time, neither of them had acknowledged openly that their relationship was anything more than a valuable and worthwhile friendship. Now they came face to face with the truth that they loved each other but had no leading from God about a future together. Elisabeth believed she would be going to Africa as a missionary, and Jim to South America. Neither perceived any leading from God to dissuade them from these paths, so it was difficult to understand how a love for each other could be fulfilled through traditional courtship and marriage.

They walked and talked in the evenings. One night, they wandered through a gateway and into a cemetery. As they sat on a rock, Jim told Elisabeth that he had committed her to God in a sacrificial way. That night he wrote: "Came to an understanding at the Cross with Betty last night. Seemed the Lord made me think of it as laying a sacrifice on the altar. She has put her life there, and I almost felt as if I would lay a hand on it, to retrieve it for myself, but it is not mine—wholly God's. He paid for it and is worthy to do with it what He will."[7]

They sat in silence that night, aware that the rising moon had cast the shadow of a great stone cross between them.

Elisabeth was a year ahead of Jim and Dave in school, so her graduation arrived in the spring of 1948, shortly after this experience in the cemetery. Dave was dating a woman who was also graduating that year. Around the time of graduation, Dave would often go see Phyllis late in the evening to say good night. When he returned to the dorm the first night, he encountered Jim on his way out. He did not think much of it at the time, though it was unusual for Jim to go out at night. When Dave asked Jim where he was going, Jim simply replied, "To talk to your sister."

The same thing happened the next night, and the night after that. This went on for a week. By then the pattern was clear, and Dave realized that these late-night meetings were not simply casual conversations with a friend's sister. Dave and Jim had been living together all during their junior year, yet only at the very end of that academic year did Dave realize that Jim had been seeing quite a lot of his sister in recent months.

During graduation week, Dave exclaimed, "For goodness' sake, Elliot, how come you never told me that you were going out with my sister every night for two weeks?"

Jim offered only a sheepish explanation. "I didn't know what to say."

Obviously, Jim was in an odd situation—with himself as much as in the eyes of other students. Ever since his arrival at Wheaton he had made such a strong point about celibacy and the call to the single life. Repeatedly, he had made other students feel inferior for going on dates. Now here he was doing the same thing. Of course, he did not know what to say.

Elisabeth graduated and left Wheaton. After that, Jim's journal became more expressive.

June 15. "Wept myself to sleep last night after seeing Betty off at the depot. Wistful all day today in spite of outdoor exercise. Feel a concentrated pressure in my throat even now. Homesickness partly—but I never felt it until after I left her. . . . The Lord gave me this affair with B.H. to try me, to see if I were really in earnest about this life of loneliness He taught me of in Matthew 19. A eunuch for the Kingdom's sake. I believe He has proved me, but I doubt if He was satisfied. I am willing to let her go but only with struggle."[8]

FOUR

Two separate passages from the Bible had led Jim and Elisabeth to believe God had called them to begin their missionary service unmarried.

Matthew 19:12 (NIV) was the basis of Jim's call: "For some are eunuchs because they were born that way; others were made that way by men; and others have renounced marriage because of the kingdom of heaven. The one who can accept this should accept it."

Elisabeth's call came from Isaiah 54:5 (NASB), "Your husband is your Maker, whose name is the LORD of Hosts," and from 1 Corinthians 7:34–35 (NIV), "An unmarried woman or virgin is concerned about the Lord's affairs: Her aim is to be devoted to the Lord in both body and spirit. But a married woman is concerned about the affairs of this world—how she can please her husband. I am saying this for your own good, not to restrict you, but that you may live in a right way in undivided devotion to the Lord."

Although he had a reputation for openly saying he would be a "eunuch for the kingdom," and indeed he was prepared to be single if that is how he could best serve the Lord, Jim Elliot was aware of his own physical nature. He was a man, and he was attracted to a woman.

Elisabeth struggled similarly. She longed for someone to love, and also to be loved. These feelings intensified after she began a friendship with Jim Elliot. Yet she was sure of her call to the mission field—Africa, not South America where Jim was headed.

Why God would give them this strong sense of call and then seemingly test it by giving them a love for each other was a mystery to them both.

After her graduation, Elisabeth went to the University of Oklahoma to spend the summer studying linguistics. Like Jim, she hoped someday to work with deciphering an unwritten language and reducing its sounds to an alphabet of some sort. Wycliffe, a mission organization known for its linguistic work among primitive tribes, offered an intensive course in Oklahoma for both experienced missionaries and those who had not yet been overseas. It was the next step in Elisabeth's preparation to go to Africa—and seemingly a step farther away from Jim.

Longing for Jim went with Elisabeth on that train ride across middle America. She found she could hardly think, read, or pray about anything except Jim Elliot. Jim's brother Bert, who later went as a missionary to Peru, was also at the University of Oklahoma that summer. His profile, his singing, his demeanor, all reminded Elisabeth of Jim. While she appreciated the opportunity to get to know a member of Jim's family—she had not met any of them before—Bert's presence was also a reminder of Jim's absence.

While Elisabeth studied, Jim spent a good part of the summer traveling with a team representing the Foreign Missions Fellowship, as he had done on other occasions. His companions included his good friend Dave Howard and two other students, and their journey took them across the northern Midwest, from Michigan to Montana. They spoke in churches, Bible conferences, camps, and schools. Their particular emphasis on this trip was to persuade young people of the urgency of missionary work to tribes who had never heard of Christ.

At times, they wondered if the trip was worth the effort. For instance, when they arrived in Port Huron, Michigan, only a few days after leaving Wheaton, they faced the discouragement of a small place and few opportunities to speak to students. But not every stop was so disheartening. When the trip was over, Jim himself commented: "The month's trip is over, and I trust Eternity will reveal fruit for the effort. I have not known before such freedom in ministering. Surely prayer has been heard and answered."[1]

Giving talks to encourage interest in missions is an activity in which success is difficult to measure. Even if a large crowd attends the presentation, and even if dozens of people express willingness to consider a future in missions, how can a speaker know how much lasting impact has been achieved? On the other hand, at a small gathering where only a few individuals consider missions, someone may make a life-long commitment that will eventually result in reaching hundreds of people.

Years later, Dave Howard reflected that Jim had preached with a rare passion and effectiveness that summer. Students in many of the places where they preached began preparing for missionary service. Jim seemed to have a persuasive gift for stirring people up.

Jim and Elisabeth had agreed not to write to each other during that summer. In September of 1948, just before Jim began his last year of college, they had a chance to be together in Wheaton for almost a week. They took long walks, visited with Jim's aunt in nearby Glen Ellyn, and visited the Lagoon where they had admitted their love for each other. As their visit drew to a close, Jim wrote, "I hope earnestly I have not grieved the Holy Dove in all this. I really feel quite happy in my soul, yet dare not trust this treacherous heart. O Father, if I am not pleasing Thee, give me unrest and deep conviction. I feel now that our love is truly 'in the Spirit,' but I would not have false peace, not even if I got her, Lord!"[2]

And the next day his struggle continued. "Woke this morning with thoughts from Acts 5 about holding back part of the price. Ananias and Sapphira were not slain for not giving, but for not giving everything as they said they would. How can I know my heart as regards Betty? I cannot."[3]

His struggle continued, yet his affection for Elisabeth persisted to the point that others became aware of it. He wrote to his parents about Elisabeth right after that September visit. He boasted of her "deliciously satisfying company," and assured them that his attraction had nothing to do with her physical features. In fact, he described her as having little appeal in terms of physical attraction. Instead, though, her thought patterns were like his in thousands of details, and he had never experienced that in a relationship before. They were kindred spirits and they both knew it, but they were afraid to admit it.[4]

Here, Jim revealed to his parents the conflict they both felt. They had committed themselves to God for mission work, and believed He intended they should begin their work as single adults. Their like-mindedness was an impediment to love, rather than an encouragement. Moreover, God was leading them to two different continents. They had discovered that they were kindred spirits. But such a relationship seemed to have no place in their lives, at least at that point in time.

They talked about marriage, but it seemed as if needing each other in that way might mean that they felt Christ was not sufficient for them. And neither of them seemed to want to consider that possibility: it would be a weakness inconsistent with their goals of becoming missionaries. They did not exclude the possibility that they might someday marry, but it would have to be under circumstances that were exactly right. If they were to marry, if would be as a gift from Christ. First, they must be sure He was sufficient for all their needs, including that of love.

In October 1948, following the September visit, they began to correspond, though their letters were infrequent. While Jim remained at Wheaton for his senior year of college, Elisabeth went to Alberta, Canada, to a Bible school. Elisabeth wrote postcards and mailed them from train stops along the way. Jim responded in his journal: "Card from Betty just now written from Moose Jaw.

Got one Wednesday from Saint Paul with just two words, 'Miss you,' and today only one, 'More.' I fear that the excitement of her presence roused me to an aggressiveness in my ardor that I do not really feel. O Lord, let me deal tenderly with her."[5]

Elisabeth's simple, sparse words communicated volumes about what she was feeling—and evoked a curious response from Jim. In May he had been overt about his emotions. Now, in October, he was more guarded.

Jim's first letter to Elisabeth arrived in Canada on October 4, and his words reflected his continuing struggle to understand his feelings and relationship with Elisabeth. He wrote to her about his struggle. He recognized that he wanted her in his life, but he did not want her as she wanted him. Pleasing God with a single missionary life and having Elisabeth were two conflicting desires.[6]

In his last year of college, it was natural for Jim to wonder about what he would be doing a year from that time. Most college seniors face that question. His journal from November of 1948 reflects several options. He could go to Peru as a missionary, following his brother Bert's example, or go to India, on the basis of a recent interest in that country. A third option was to go to Europe and work in college camps, teaching the Bible. This had been suggested by an InterVarsity leader, but Jim saw it as improbable. He could return to Wheaton to pursue another degree in biblical literature, but he was not eager to continue the academic life. Although gifted intellectually, he was not persuaded it was always the best preparation for pioneer missionary work.

Pondering these options, none of which seemed the

least bit clear, and none of which included Elisabeth, Jim wrote: "Lead on, Lord. If none of these is Your plan, Your revelation must be seen."[7] It was not Jim's nature to choose something for lack of a better choice. He continued to wait.

Even without clear leading, however, Jim's movement to the mission field continued unthwarted, either by romance or by parental pressure. In November 1948 Jim wrote to his mother, chiding her for trying to influence him. He had no intention of getting fat "leaning on pulpits."[8]

Jim was the president of the Student Foreign Missions Fellowship at Wheaton College during his senior year. By now, he was well known and influential on campus. Two years earlier, he had attended the first InterVarsity missionary convention in Toronto with his friend Dave Howard. InterVarsity carries out a ministry to students on university campuses and encourages interest in mission work. Gathered at that convention were 575 students, which seemed like a huge gathering on the theme of missions to Jim and Dave.

InterVarsity considered it successful enough to try again in a more central location, such as the University of Illinois at Urbana, Illinois. Nearly thirteen hundred students attended the second convention, Jim and Dave among them. In fact, as the president of Student Foreign Missionary Fellowship at Wheaton, Jim organized about one hundred students to go to Urbana between Christmas and New Year's in 1948.

As Jim anticipated the convention, he wrote, "Lord, show me what Thine intent is regarding these meetings that I might pray according to the will of God."[9]

Jim did more than simply attend the convention. Drawing on the dramatic talent of his youth, Jim presented a spectacular drama during the convention. Not originally part of the program, the drama was presented during the afternoons. Jim had written it himself and presented it in a way that allowed other students to be involved. Jim narrated while others acted out symbolically scenes that showed what God was doing in mission fields around the world.

Jim's preparation for the event influenced him profoundly, although he had mixed feelings about the outcome of the convention as a whole. He wrote to his parents that he had come expecting a time of deep heart-searching, with lives being turned over to unseen treasures. On the one hand, during the convention he became certain in his own mind that the Lord wanted him to go to South America. He felt the Lord's presence in prayer and was more certain of his own future. But in his view, God had not taken hold of the group as a whole. Too many people lacked an intense feeling about answering God's call.[10]

As Jim pondered the potential gathered under the roof of the convention—from Anglican priests and a Mennonite bishop, to American students and veteran missionaries—he wondered how long they would all sit around analyzing and discussing before God would take hold of them with power and thrust them out into the places in the world where Christ was unknown.

If this did not happen on a wide scale at the convention, it did happen for Jim. And the end of the convention he wrote, "The Lord has done what I wanted Him to do for me this week. I wanted primarily a peace about going into pioneer Indian work. As I analyze my feelings now, I am quite at ease about saying that tribal work in the South American jungle is the general direction of my missionary purpose. Also, I am confident that God wants me to begin jungle work single."[11]

Did this mean any change in Jim's relationship with Elisabeth? No. He wrote, "God has led us together in writing, and I have no sign that His will is anything else than that we continue."[12] That status quo would continue. Older men, experienced missionaries, had advised him that there were many jobs on the mission field that could not be accomplished by a man encumbered with responsibilities to a wife and family. The mission field needed single men to pioneer in these areas. Jim was ready to be a pioneer.

Elisabeth, in turn, feared that she might become the distraction that would turn Jim away from doing just this. She questioned whether they even ought to be corresponding. Would it not be better if Jim simply focused on discerning God's will regarding what country he would go to? Even though they had made no formal or public commitment to each other, she wanted to be sure their relationship would not become a liability to him.

Jim wrote in his journal: "January 17. Stung with a regret that almost brings me to sobbing as I received Betty's letter of the twelfth. I wrote carelessly that I felt God was leading me singly to the field, and it has touched her far more deeply than I supposed. Oh God, how can she desire me? Have I played the part so well that she actually thinks me worthy of woman's love?"[13]

If waiting for direction from God was difficult, Jim put the lesson to good use. He came to understand that "one does not surrender a life in an instant—that which is lifelong can only be surrendered in a lifetime. I can only surrender to the will of God as I know what that will is. This may take years to know."[14]

FIVE

A strange thing happened during the spring semester of 1949. The shell around Jim Elliot be-gan to crack. As Jim wrestled with the sober issues of his future—and failed to find answers—he started to change in ways that shocked even himself—and later Elisabeth. He later referred to this time of his life as his "renaissance."

Jim had arrived at Wheaton with a strong code of "don'ts." The Foreign Missions Fellowship students that he socialized with—as much as he socialized with anyone—were a serious group. One student in particular, Bill Cathers, was much like Jim in his spiritual outlook. It was important to both of them to use their time wisely, edify themselves, and minister to others spiritually, and in general focus their energy on the mission work that lay ahead of them.

But in the spring of 1949, both Jim and Bill started to see things differently. It now seemed to them that the austere attitudes they had adopted for themselves were inconsistent with the apostle Paul's teaching about the freedom of the Christian. They looked around at students engaged in a range of activities that they themselves had shunned. But now they saw that they did not have to evaluate everything according to how "spiritual" it was. Some things were simply good clean fun that built friendships for the future. Jim wrote: "[Bill Cathers] and my thoughts regarding false spiritual standards we FMFs have established among ourselves coincide in that we feel perfect liberty in doing things which we [in our minds] condemned before."[1]

Jim now believed that "God has given us richly all things to enjoy." Bill Cathers had always had a strong influence on Jim, and together they now entered into a new phase. God was bigger than they had previously thought. Jim realized that he had been depriving himself of some of the blessings which God had given him to enjoy richly. His outgoing, fun-loving personality had been held back for years. Sometimes he had even felt guilty for not harnessing his inclinations to humor and pranks even more tightly. With the onset of his renaissance, the stops came out, and the pendulum swung in the other direction. Jim never did anything in a halfhearted way. If he was going to enjoy life, he would enjoy it tremendously. Bible study and prayer, though still playing a major role in his daily routine, did not have to consume every spare moment.

Jim entered into college activities with a new liberty, one that let him enjoy them for the pleasure they brought, not only for their spiritual value. He began to enjoy life and to enter into good-spirited fun.

For instance, Jim had always participated on

Wheaton's wrestling squad because it was building up his body for the rigors of pioneer mission work. Now he wrestled also because it was fun and because he was good at it. In fact, with this new attitude, he got better. Winning, which had never mattered before, now was important. And he did win more.

Another change Jim made was to start eating in the Upper Dining Hall. The Lower Dining Hall, where he had been eating all through college, was less expensive and patronized by students with a reputation for being serious and spiritually minded. This had seemed to fit Jim's profile. Now, in the Upper Dining hall, Jim encountered a broader spectrum of his fellow students. He saw that rather than ministering to other students in earlier years, he had been cutting himself off from them. He had been going about his objective all wrong. Rather than create an artificial barrier between himself and other students based on his judgments of their spirituality, it would be more effective to mingle with them and experience life alongside them. He had a greater influence on other students now that they viewed him as part of normal life, rather than as an eccentric recluse or monk.

Jim began to go to class parties and football and basketball games. He entered into the traditional rivalry between the junior and senior classes at Wheaton. His wild side was released, and he was uncharacteristically involved in pranks, such as throwing the junior class president into the lake, or tying him up on a flagpole, or turning his room upside down.

Jim had a classmate, Ed McCully, who was talented dramatically and competed on a national level in oratory skills. Jim had had a dramatic bent since his boyhood, and now he expressed it in cahoots with Ed.

The two of them conjured up a very convincing drunken act. They would go out in public and board a bus hanging all over each other and talking very loudly and generally causing a commotion. Understandably, people would move away from them on the bus. But Jim and Ed kept their faces straight and stayed in their roles. Their lines went like this:

Ed: Hey, Jim, did I ever tell you about the three kinds of love?

Jim: No. Tell me about the three kinds of love.

Ed: First there's the love of a man for his wife. Then there's the love of a mother for her baby. But there's no love like the love of one drunken bum for another drunken bum.

Traditionally, the senior class of Wheaton College would sneak away for a weekend during their last semester, a time known as Senior Sneak. The junior class would try to discover their destination and steal their luggage en route. If the senior class reached their camp with their luggage intact, they had succeeded in their Sneak.

The class of 1949 was successful in foiling the juniors. But the fun at Egg Harbor, Wisconsin, was just beginning, and Jim was in the middle of it.

Ed McCully, who was the class president, missed the beginning of the weekend because he had been in San Francisco, California, where he had won the national oratory contest. Dave Howard drove down to Green

Bay, Wisconsin, and picked him up and drove back to join the Sneak. The class was waiting to congratulate Ed on his national victory—and promptly threw him in the lake.

Then the women went after Jim. He was attractive and personable and had emerged from the class as a natural leader. But his reputation for being uninterested in women persisted. No one knew about his relationship with Elisabeth Howard. For his indifference, the girls wanted to throw Jim in the lake. If he did not want anything to do with them, they would let him know how they felt about that. Eight or ten of the women tackled him. Rubberneck Elliot squirmed out and escaped, but a male classmate came to the aid of the women and tackled him. They dragged him down to the water and threw him in. He paid the price for his well-earned reputation.

The water games did not end there. The men raided the women's cabin at night, armed with water guns, and soaked all the beds. Jim was in the thick of it, along with Dave and Ed. One of the women was so mad, she whacked every one of them on the head with a high-heeled shoe on their way out.

Of course, Jim's serious side did not fade away. Also during the days of the hilarious Senior Sneak, he and Ed McCully led a breaking of bread service in the traditional Plymouth Brethren style of common loaf and common cup. After a few opening comments, Ed and Jim led in prayers and familiar hymns. Ed broke the bread and gave thanks for the cup, and then the single cup was passed around, Brethren style, to about 180 people attending the Sneak.

When it was all over, Jim did his best to put every-thing into balanced perspective. He was still looking for spiritual profit and was indecisive about what had come from the Sneak experience. He had had a lot of fun and gotten to know other students on a spiritual plane he had not seen before. He knew that the communion service had been truly worshipful for the senior class. But why could the Spirit not be present among them more often?[2]

Back on campus, though, the fun continued. Jim still had some things to get out of his system. Ed McCully gave his national award-winning oratory presentation on campus for students to hear. Jim and Ed and others had dates to go on as a group after the recital. Jim, who had not dated before his senior year except for one discreet and spiritual date with Elisabeth, was comfortable enough in a group setting. The men decided to take their dates for a walk in a cemetery, although the women were reluctant. They struck up a conversation about two criminals who had recently escaped from DuPage County Jail, saying that they had heard they had been seen in the area. The women were duly unsettled by this notion, which of course encouraged the men.

Suddenly, a fight broke out, and they could hear the thwacks and punches of two men on the far side of a clump of bushes. Two distinct voices argued and threat-ened loudly. The students stood speechless and motion-less, rattled by the commotion. Was it possible that the escaped criminals actually had come to this quiet, sub-urban cemetery? The fighting continued.

Then a gun went off. A body flopped to the ground in the shadows not far from the Wheaton students. The other guy darted off across the dark cemetery.

"Let's go catch him!" Jim called out, and the men sprinted after the man who had fired the gun and fled. Horrified, the women locked arms back to back in a circle so that it would be impossible for someone to get behind any one of them. The night seemed interminable. Every stirring breeze struck terror in their hearts.

Finally, the men returned, bemoaning the fact that they had not been able to catch the criminal and unconcerned about the fearful state of their dates. Jim then insisted that his date, Murial, who was a nurse, should tend to the man who had been shot and had fallen. She was reluctant, but at Jim's insistence, she bent over the still form to examine him. The man had fallen face down, and it was dark. When he started shaking, she decided he was in shock and no doubt frightened half to death. Seeing that he was a very young man, Murial leaned down and whispered in his ear, "It's going to be all right, sonny boy." She patted his head to try to relax him.

Jim then insisted that they should take the wounded man to the hospital and that Murial should ride in the back seat of the car to look after him on the way. Once they were in the car and on the way, the driver switched on the dome light. To Murial's shock, the fallen man popped up and said, "Hello, Murial."

Jim and Ed (who had done both voices during the staged fight) and the others had gone to great lengths to set up the entire prank, and had succeeded.

Jim's fun did not distract him from his ultimate purpose. As president of the Foreign Missions Fellowship, Jim had organized a group of missionary candidates to pray specifically for other students on campus who were not yet thinking about missionary work. They each selected five campus leaders and prayed that God would call them to worldwide missionary service. One of the people Jim picked out was Ed McCully, senior class president, star end on the football team, who held the college record in the 220-yard dash, winner of a national oratory contest—and who was planning to be a lawyer, not a missionary. Ed was brilliant, smooth, suave, impressive, a great speaker. Anyone could see that he would make a great lawyer.

Shortly after Ed had won the national oratory championship, Jim and Dave were coming into the locker room one day after a workout in the gymnasium. Ed was finishing up another athletic activity at the same time. In his brusque, forthright way, Jim grabbed Ed by the neck and said, "Hey, McCully, so you won the national oratory contest. Great stuff, McCully. You have a lot of talent, don't you? Where'd you get that ability? You know where you got it. God gave it to you. So what are you going to do with it, McCully? Spend it on yourself all your life making money for yourself? You have no business doing that. You ought to be a missionary. I'm praying that God will make you one."

Dave, who was also planning to be a missionary, stood by, looking sheepish at Jim's uninhibited speech. Who was Jim to point a finger at Ed McCully so brashly and tell him what he should do with his future?

Ed McCully went to law school.

SIX

The future was still one big question mark. Jim graduated from Wheaton, not knowing yet what his next step would be. His dedication to study had paid off, and he had graduated with honors and emerged as an influential student leader. Onlookers no doubt would have said that he was a young man with a bright future. He should have been plunging into some activity that would begin an illustrious career. At the very least, he could have embarked on a distinguished form of Christian ministry. Instead, he drove across the country and moved back in with his parents, with no apparent plans for anything.

The long-range future of going to South America was clear, but Jim did not know to which country he would go, or even when. He had no idea how long it would be before he left for this unknown destination. His only immediate plans were to go home to Portland and help his brother Bob build a house. His brother Bert had married and had already left as a missionary to Peru, while Jim was left in limbo, both in terms of his own future and in his relationship with Elisabeth.

One challenge he had to overcome before he could begin missionary service was to gain the support of the loosely organized Plymouth Brethren assemblies. Jim could have presented himself to a more established and structured missionary-sending board, which might have sped up the process for him, but he chose to remain within his own tradition. Gaining the approval he needed would take time. He could not go until he received a "commendation" from his local assembly. And he could not receive a commendation until he had a clear call where he would go. And even a commendation was no guarantee of financial support.

On July 8, 1949, only a few weeks after leaving college, Jim recorded in his journal, "Mingled feelings of 'not belonging' and of thanksgiving for all God's grace these past four years. God, preserve me from living a life which conforms to the general pattern. To whom shall I go for counsel for a way of life? To whom for example? To Thee, Lord? Yea, I come to Thee."[1]

One of Jim's first tasks was to help paint the assembly hall where his family worshiped in Portland, Oregon. By all appearances, this was mundane work, but, following his old habits, Jim did his best to redeem even this time. He wrote to his friend Bill Cathers about standing on a scaffold with his father and discussing effective methods for preparing young men for the Lord's work.[2]

He wrote to Elisabeth recounting his ordinary activities: fixing the car, cleaning up the meeting hall, painting the house, and unsnarling the city's red tape that had delayed construction on his brother's house. Recognizing how easy it would be to lag spiritually in such a setting, and fraught with frustration at not being overseas, Jim tried to take a longer view. He reconciled himself to staying in the United States until he had proven himself in the assemblies there. He remained confident that eventually the Lord would make the way clear for him to go to South America.

It was a daily struggle, though. Only a few days after writing to Elisabeth of this confidence, Jim recorded in his journal, "Restless to do other things more directly related to the Lord's work. Oh, there is time to read and seek God, but my desire slackens."[3]

In September of 1949, the horizon brightened with a visit from Elisabeth, who was working with the Canadian Sunday School Mission in a rural part of Alberta, Canada. Her parents had sent her money for a visit home, and at the same time, Jim's mother had persistently invited Elisabeth to visit the Elliot family in Portland. Although Jim had met Elisabeth's family during the Christmas visit in 1947, Elisabeth had met only Jim's brother Bert during her linguistic studies in Oklahoma. She had never met Jim's parents. She debated about accepting the invitation and finally decided to visit the Elliots on her way home to her family. She was so nervous, she barely moved a muscle while she sat on the bus from Seattle to Portland.

The days in Portland were full and rich. The first few days were consumed with meetings at the Gospel Hall at an annual Labor Day conference. The Elliot men were heavily involved as speakers and hosts. Jim and Elisabeth had little opportunity for private conversation. Elisabeth

could not help wondering—hoping against hope—
whether Jim had any clearer leading about the future of
their relationship. She hoped he did, but no, his only response came from Isaiah 59:9 (NIV): "We look for light,
but all is darkness; for brightness, but we walk in deep
shadows." They would continue to wait.

One morning, Elisabeth was helping Mrs. Elliot
with the laundry, and the older woman said, "I know
these Elliot men. They can never make up their minds.
If I were you I'd tell Jim it's now or never."[4]

This Elisabeth could not do. She had no doubt in her
mind that if she gave Jim such an ultimatum, his answer
would be a certain "Never," and Elisabeth did not want to
cut off every possibility of hope. She maintained her restrained, patient position, holding herself back from ex-
pressing her feelings fully and trusting that Jim's reasons
for not making a commitment to her were more worthy
than simply an inherited trait of indecision.

They discussed marriage during that visit, and not
just theoretically, but marriage to each other. In Jim's
mind, marriage and Elisabeth had become synonymous.
If he were to be married at all, it would be to Elisabeth.
They prayed together for the first time, and Jim spent
money on Elisabeth for the very first time. Their relationship was taking a turn, but it was still without definite
direction.

They parted again, with no commitment to the future, no promises of when they would see each other
again. They would be separated by most of a continent
during an era when long-distance telephone calls were
rare, much less frequent transcontinental air travel. Jim
wrote in his journal: "She has been gone one hour. What

thunders of feelings I have known in that short time. I could not read the neon lights as I turned away from the bus and couldn't face the people as they passed me. Leaving her is terrible. Each time I see her, I have no answer. Only that I must wait. How long? For what? I know not."[5]

It was during this same month, September of 1949, that Elisabeth's brother and Jim's friend, David Howard, decided to take the plunge and became engaged. He wrote to Jim with the news, and Jim replied promptly.

> *Your mother had written Betty when she was here of your first intimations of action when she asked you clean out of a clear sky about Phyl. Betty and I prayed over the matter together and then, in the muddles of my own wonderings over Betty, I had forgotten that action might be impending. Somehow, Dave, it doesn't seem at all incongruous, in spite of all we have said about Phyl hardly being a fit for you. Time was when I would have gone berserk to think of you pulling such a rash stunt, but I am learning slowly not to be surprised when the Lord takes a notion to cause winds to blow in the mulberries.*

Jim's letter then turned to Elisabeth's recent visit.

> *Betty and I had a couple of very enjoyable days together in the open, one on Mt. Hood and another at the beach. Nothing short of terrific, brother. We had several afternoon outings, canoeing one day, swimming another, and just lying around on the slopes of our tiny volcano, Mt.*

Tabor, talking over our letters. I like her more than ever, now, and on a little different basis than before. Sorry I have no news for you as startling as you put in your last. Her coming here, however, has put fresh problems on the stage.

My folks' attitude is the most prominent of these. I don't know how she managed to do it, but Betty left the worst impressions possible upon the family. Imagine my having to defend Betty on charges of unfriendliness and uncommunicativeness. Betty Howard uncommunicative! She can talk the leg off a brass donkey ordinarily, but she betrayed so independent an attitude here that no one believes me. Of course, none of them realized entirely what a difficult position she was in coming to my home with practically no introduction. She flunked the social test among the assembly folks, and they swear that they tried to make conversation. It would worry me a mite if I didn't believe for certain that the Lord led her as definitely as ever He led any. What He was allowing in letting her give such terrible impressions, I don't know, but I hear constantly rumbles of Mom's and Dad's dissatisfaction in table conversation. How she'll ever make it good, I don't know, but I sense barriers.

Our relationship is still undefined; we left each other in silence again—for the third time. It was the worst time for me, and I suspect for her, too, although I haven't had a letter since she left. Frankly, I don't have a clear conscience about going on like this, to say nothing of the misery I

personally experience in seeing her go, with no
promises of hope as far as we know now. It is
enough, however, to walk one step at a time, and
the revealed step for me is: No prospects of mar-
riage (or engagement) until the field is settled on.

Jim continued doing odd jobs for the remaining fall months and contemplating how the Lord was molding him spiritually for the challenges ahead of him. He read the diaries and biographies of great missionaries, such as David Brainerd, Jonathan Goforth, and Hudson Taylor. Inspired by their faith, he longed for God to grant him grace to imitate their faith.

He took particular encouragement from reading about the last months of Brainerd's life. Jim was struck by the value of leading a godly life in light of the possibility of an early death. In the wake of World War II, which had claimed the lives of so many young men, pondering an early death was understandable. Even if his life was to be short, Jim wanted it to be his best effort at being in fellowship with God.

During this time, Jim kept up with his correspondence. The first letter he received from Elisabeth after her visit accused him of being only half-heartedly sorry for some of the shenanigans of his renaissance during his last year of college. From her perspective, he had gone too far in the name of enjoying the freedom God has given. He also received a letter from Dave, Elisabeth's brother, exhorting him to stop stirring up love in Elisabeth by continuing to write to her without commitment.

A few days later, Jim read a letter written to his brother Bert, now in Peru, from a missionary in Ecuador.

Dr. Wilfred Tidmarsh outlined the needs for mission work among the Quichua Indian tribe of Ecuador. Dr. Tidmarsh was going to have to leave the work because of his wife's ill health. He had asked another mission group to take over the mission station, but so far he had received no decision. If a replacement was not found, the investment of many years of work would go untended. Jim's first impulse was to write and offer himself for that work, and he did so. However, before he mailed the letter, he realized that he had been presumptuous in taking such action without some definite word from the Lord that his future lay in Ecuador. He set the letter aside and kept waiting.

At the end of October, Jim took some action toward finding a job. He applied as a substitute teacher. He also began to seek more opportunities for ministry. He helped out in a new class for unsaved children in an assembly in suburban Portland and conducted Wednesday afternoon meetings for children in his own assembly hall. He held evangelistic street meetings.

In November Jim reflected on his thoughts of a year earlier, when he had pondered what he might be doing at that point in his life. He discovered that of all the options he had listed the previous year, he was engaged in none. Within himself he was content because he believed he should not undertake any activity unless directed by the Lord to do so, and the Lord had not led in any of the directions Jim had anticipated.

By December 1949, however, Jim was aware of the rumblings around him. The rumor reached his ears that people were talking about him. Six months had passed since his graduation from college. Why was he not doing something more substantial than odd jobs, substitute teaching, and random evangelistic activities? Some felt that he ought to get a job; what they did not know was that he had applied for three jobs recently but had been offered none of them. His work keeping up the assembly hall seemed unappreciated, and his habits of withdrawing for long periods of reading and meditation—up to eight hours a day—were misunderstood. Naturally his impulse was to defend himself. But he did not. Instead, he knelt and prayed, renewing his commitment to be satisfied with nothing less than throwing himself into the hands of God.

A few weeks later, Jim wrote to Elisabeth with information that showed he was at last finding a clearer focus on a specific mission field. He had, after all, corresponded with Wilfred Tidmarsh in Ecuador. He had also written to Rowland Hill in India. Both fields were of tremendous interest to Jim, but the work was very different. In Ecuador, the works were among a primitive, illiterate tribe, while in India the project involved high school- and college-age Hindus studying English. Rowland Hill wanted to start a Bible school and was looking for a Greek teacher. Jim received an invitation to join the India work the next year. Jim was certainly well qualified. But still he waited.

On the last night of 1949, Jim wrote, "Moved to sober prayer again after reading Tidmarsh's moving letter of December 26. Oh, Lord, You see the places secret in me. If You see anything in me that is holding back the clear revelation of Your will about Ecuador, uncover it to me, I pray. If it is Your mind that I should go there, then send me—soon."[6]

A letter from Jim Elliot to David Howard after David had announced his engagement and after Elizabeth had visited Jim in Portland.

PS. ept26, 1949..
7272 S.E.Thorburn
Portland, Cregon

THE LORD HATH DONE WHAT HE PLEASEDIN HEAVEN AND EARTH
Psalm 135:6

This verse was in my Psalm reading this noon after
getting word of your recent move, David. It was sign
sufficient to me to show me what attitude I should
take toward your new relationship with Phyl. Wisdom
of God! Who can understand His secrets, for surely
He has treasured up for Himself the ways of His be-
loved, and this union, unpredicted and improbable
from my point of view is another notice that as the
heavens are high above the earth so are my thoughts
higher than your thots, saith the Lord.

Your mother had written Betty when she was here of
your first intimations of action when she asked you
clean out of a clear skyabout Phyl when you had been
praying for some sign of that sort. / Betty and
I prayed over the matter together and then, in the
muddles of my own wonderings over Bet ty, I had for-
gotten that action might be impending. Somehow, Dave,
it doesn't seem at all incongrous,. in spite of all
we have said about Phyl hardly being a fit for you.
Time was when I would have gone berserk to think of
you pulling such a rash stunt, but I am learning
slowly not to be surprised when the Lord takes a
notion to cause winds to blow in the mulberries . I
am glad for you both, and althoughI doubt if I shall
find occasion to tell Gibby so, I want you to congratulate her especiall y for me. I had to laugh out-
loud to think that you were almost as naive as Phil
in his love for Margaret,so that it was actually
your Mom that convinced you that you were actually
in love. Banish all care of my having any opposition
to your new relationship,as I am now behind you 100%
praying in faith and believing that
                Love knows to do
          For him, for her, from year to year
          As hitherto.

Forty of the assembly young folks from Seattle and
Portland met last Friday night up inside Mt.Ranier
Park. we slept all night in the open and on Saturday
hiked up on to the side of the mountain to the glaciers
nad explored the ice waves. Funny thing, but I can
remember thinking how much fun itwould be to have you
alcng, entering into the hugeness of the thing,
and wondering if ever we might do something like to-
             ...growing bigger in the biggness of the whole,

gether. Seems even more improbable today than it did
then. Betty and I had a couple of very enjoyable days
together in the open , one on Mt. Hood and another
at the beach...nothing short of terrific, brother.
We had several aftern oon outings, canoeing one day,
swimming another, and just lying around on the slopes
of our tiny volcano, Mt, Tabor, talking over our letters
on anothe r. I like her more than ever, now, and on
a little different basis than before. Sorry I have
no news for you as st artling as you put in your
last. Her coming here however has put fresh problems
on the stage.

M folks' attitude is the most prominent of these.
I don't know how she managed to do it, but Betty left
the worst impressions possible upon the family. Imaging
my having to defend Betty on charges of unfriendliness
and uncommunicativeness. Betty Howard uncommunicative!
She can talk the leg off a brass donkey ordinarily,
but she betrayed so independent an attitude here that
no one believes me. Of course, none of them realized
entirely what a difficult position she was in coming
to my home with practically no introduction. She flunked
the social test among the assembly folks and they
swear that they tried to make conversation. Weeeeell
it would worry me a mite if I didn't believe for certain
that The Lord led her as definitely as ever He led any.
What He was allowing in letting her give such terrible
impressions , I don't know, but I hear constantly
rumbles of Mom's and Dad's dissatisfaction in table
conversation. How she'll ever make it good , I don't
know, but I sense barriers.

Our relationship is still undefined; we left each other
in silence again-for the third time. It was the worst
time for me, and I suspect for her too, although I
haven't had a letter since she left. Frankly, I don't
have a clear conscience about going on like this, to
say nothing of the misery I personally experienced in
seeing her go...with no promises or hopes as far as
we know now. It is enough however to walk one step
at a time and the revealed step for me is: No prospects
of marraige (or engagement) until the field is settled on ,.

I hope I don't sound morbid, ad I am really very happy
in the Lord's good leading...for us both. Wonder if
we shall see one another at Homecoming. Van Nall and
Mitch are in town and have been out for supper one night.
We are going deer hunting next week end. I don't know if the
boys can get off from school or not. Still nothing!
definite for South America.
                        Gotta run ,
                          Blessings , Jim

SEVEN

The old year faded away and the new year blew in.

At a time when people traditionally make a new start, Jim Elliot continued the routine he had been following for months—living with his parents, helping out with whatever needed doing, and reading and meditating for hours at a stretch. While he did not feel that time was badly spent, waiting for a clear sign about his future was difficult. Jim was intelligent, healthy, and eager. Despite appearances, he even knew what he wanted. What he did not know was how and when he could proceed with his dreams.

For a while it seemed that going on a mission trip to British Guiana with his father was a possibility for Jim, as an interim step while waiting for the opportunity to go to a mission field on a permanent basis. But the trip to British Guiana did not materialize. Once it was clear that he would not be going there, Jim looked with more certainty toward other things. Most likely, he would spend the first half of 1950 at home in Portland. Looking beyond that, he anticipated the summer. He applied and was accepted into the linguistic program that Elisabeth had completed two years earlier. He would spend the summer in Oklahoma.

In the meantime, the Christian high school confirmed that they wanted him to conduct two weeks of student meetings. He also accepted invitations to speak in other places, such as at gatherings of nurses and medical students and at InterVarsity meetings. God was giving him an opportunity to give out some of what he had been soaking up during the months since he'd left college. The long hours of study and reflection gave him material for his talks. He did not approach these occasions unprepared, and he did not accept these invitations simply to fill time. Despite the solid framework for his talks, Jim was the worst critic of his own preaching. He thought that he was not earnest enough in the way he handled the Word of God. He chastised himself repeatedly in his journal entries. He was never quite sure whether his messages were having any effect. Years later, though, a young woman who had been a student at the high school and heard Jim speak wrote to Elisabeth and told her that, other than her parents, Jim had been the most influential person in her life; his talks from 1 Timothy during those two weeks in 1950 had profoundly impacted her spiritual development.

In February of 1950, Jim faced a decision that would commit him for the next year. The board of the Christian school where he was substituting offered him a job teaching for the next school year. They were anxious for an answer, but he was reluctant to give one. He still felt no rest about where he would be in a year's time. If he promised he would stay in Portland to teach, he might be sidetracked from the main path that God was revealing to him a few steps at a time. He asked for more time to consider the offer.

In March he faced another decision. David Howard was urging Jim to join the work of InterVarsity and Foreign Missions Fellowship. The job would mean constant travel, going into a city to speak and then leaving immediately. He would never be in one place long enough to know whether anything came of his efforts. After his experience in this kind of activity in the summer of 1948, Jim questioned whether it was effective. Although he had a persuasive personality and many considered him to be a gifted speaker, Jim was not convinced this was the right ministry for him. This sort of ministry in the United States was not foremost in his mind for the long term, so he questioned whether he ought to be involved in it even for the short term. However, it was true that he needed a job to support himself. Even living with his parents required a small income. And if he could earn some money, he might be able to put some aside for his future expenses as a missionary. But was that enough reason to take a job? In Jim's mind, it was not a good enough reason to take the wrong job.

Another drawback of the InterVarsity work was his reluctance to put himself in a position of recommending mission boards to students interested in foreign missions. He himself did not plan to go to the mission field under the guidance or authority of a mission board, so how could he convincingly suggest that others should? To do so would seem incongruous with his own nonconformist attitude toward established mission boards.

After months of being in limbo about the future, Jim now had several options for ministry in the United States. And he still felt no clear leading about a foreign field of service. What did it all mean? Was the Lord redirecting him—or testing him?

In April Jim turned down the offer by the school board for a position as a teacher. He also turned down Dave Howard and InterVarsity. No doubt he would have done well in either job, but they would contribute only to his temporary support, not his future goals. He focused instead on preparing to go to the University of Oklahoma for linguistic studies in the summer.

In Oklahoma Jim spent ten weeks, along with several hundred other new and experienced missionaries, learning how to study unwritten languages. He had to master how to write them down and analyze them. Phonetics, morphology, and syntax filled his days.

Each student worked with an "informant" to practice in a simulated field situation. Informants came from all over the world, representing various countries and languages. Their task was to provide linguistic data to students who did not know the language the informant used. Students worked individually, gathering language data and trying to organize it according to the principles they were learning.

Jim's informant was a former missionary to the Quichua Indians in the Ecuador jungle. During the course of their conversations, the missionary told Jim about an unreached tribe called the Aucas. The Aucas had repulsed, sometimes savagely, every attempt of the white man to contact them and remained untouched by modern civilization. Jim's heart lit up; this was exactly the type of mission work he longed to do.

The Ecuadorian connection caused Jim to reflect on his recent correspondence with Dr. Tidmarsh. The Quichuas themselves inhabited vast areas of land that had not been reached by missionary work. The ratio of missionaries to Quichuas was abysmal; the need was huge, and surely Jim would be welcome. The Aucas were one step beyond the Quichuas. Jim did not consider it a coincidence that he should have had a correspondence with Dr. Tidmarsh and then work with an informant from the Quichua language who had knowledge of the Aucas. He had waited too long for a sign about his future to let such simultaneous events go by. Clearly, he had to give Ecuador some serious thought.

Jim took a brief break from his studies—and his contemplations—in Oklahoma to drive to Wheaton with a group of friends to attend David Howard's wedding, which, of course, gave him an opportunity to see Elisabeth as well. David and Phyllis Howard were married in Wheaton and then drove to nearby Chicago for a festive dinner; they planned to stay in a hotel in Chicago for the night. Jim, who was their best man, and about twenty other friends from their college years joined the celebration in Chicago.

After dinner, as David and Phyllis were being escorted by a bellhop to their room, a fight broke out around the corner of the hall they were in. They could hear punches and grunts and mutterings, and the bellhop was visibly concerned about what they had encountered. Suddenly, one of the fighters came flying around the corner and landed on his back on the floor in front of them. The bellhop bolted for a telephone to call hotel security.

"Don't bother," Dave told him. "We know these guys." At his feet was his old classmate, Ed McCully; the assailant around the corner was Jim Elliot. Both of them were enjoying themselves immensely.

Dave and Phyllis found the room where they would spend their wedding night. No doubt to their surprise, so did their twenty friends. Jim boldly led the entourage into the room, stirring up boisterous behavior and a lively party atmosphere.

Understandably, after a few minutes, Dave was ready for this gang to leave. But Jim was the influential personality in the room. Knowing Jim as well as he did, Dave strategized and decided that the way to get Jim to sober up his behavior was to ask him to read from the Bible. This he did, and Jim readily agreed.

Dave had in mind that Jim would read a few verses to change the tone in the room and then leave. Jim had in mind reading a few chapters for serious edification. He opened up a Bible and read all six chapters of 1 Timothy. Then he turned to the twenty friends crammed into the room and asked for their reflections on the meaning of what he had read. When they hesitated, he embarked on a long discourse of his own, which lasted for nearly an hour. Finally, he announced that they should pray for each other. Many of them were students who had graduated one or two years earlier and had not seen each other in a long time. Jim thought it would be worthwhile to take advantage of being together to catch up on news of their activities so they could pray for each other.

After two or three people had shared their recent activities, someone had the good sense to suggest that Jim close in prayer and they would all leave.

Dave and Phyllis were finally left on their own.

Jim realized later he had gotten carried away. He wrote in his journal: "My own volatility was manifest after the wedding and my loss of spiritual potency as well. Warned, I did not watch and fell into folly. Saw Betty again with joy and refreshment. She was faithful in rebuking me for my loss of dignity and manifest crudeness."[1]

Later, Jim wrote a letter to Dave apologizing for his behavior on the night of the wedding. Interestingly, his apology was confined to the boisterous partying, such as the fight in the hall, and touched not at all on the lengthy Bible study and prayer session held in the hotel room where the bridal couple had been ready to be left alone! Dave puzzled about this more than once after Jim's apology. Dave went so far as to ask Elisabeth if she thought Jim was truly oblivious to the fact that Bible study and prayer in someone else's honeymoon room was not a welcome gesture. This seemed quite believable for Jim Elliot.

Returning to Oklahoma, Jim had to get back to the business of his own future. He had decided to set aside ten days to spend praying for God's clear guidance about whether he was to go to Ecuador. With him in Oklahoma was his college friend Bill Cathers, who was also interested in mission work in Ecuador. During this time, Jim prayed three times a day, hoping that at the end of that time he would know whether he should write to Tidmarsh again. He shared these prayers with Bill and another friend, each promising that they would say nothing to anyone else about their spiritual exercise. Jim also spent these days gathering more information about the Quichuas. He learned that the highland Quichuas were one of the neediest mission fields, with only five missionaries for 800,000 Quichuas. One missionary gave the trio a sketch of the areas of need, including the Quichuas and the unreached Aucas.

On July 14, ten days after embarking on concentrated prayer concerning Ecuador, Jim was reading Exodus 23 (KJV). Two verses leaped out at him. "Behold, I send an Angel before thee, to keep thee in the way, and to bring thee into the place which I have prepared. Beware of him, and obey his voice." Jim took this as a sign that he should write to Dr. Tidmarsh of his willingness to come to Ecuador. Together, he and his college friend Bill Cathers wrote to Dr. Tidmarsh and to assembly elders in Portland and Wheaton. Jim wrote in his journal with certainty: "God is sending me there."[2]

A couple of weeks later, Jim wrote to his parents telling them how the pieces of the puzzle had come together. He was ready to go immediately, waiting only for the decision of the elders in Portland. He still needed their blessing in the form of an official commendation.

Jim's parents and others still questioned the decision, wondering whether his ministry should be in the United States, stirring up young people as he had been doing. They believed his gifts for Bible teaching and preaching were unusual gifts, and he would be very effective in fueling the passion for missions among other people who would go.

Jim would have none of it. Since his brother Bert was

already in Peru as a missionary, he understood his parents' sense of loss at the prospect of a second son moving to another continent. He wrote to his parents, rebuking their reluctance to see him go. They should instead be rejoicing that the will of God was being done.[3]

In early August, Jim received word from the leaders of the Portland assembly that he should feel that the assembly was behind him in going to Ecuador. "God has set His seal," Jim recorded in his journal.

Bill Cathers was also heading toward Ecuador. Of course, this encouraged Jim. Jim had admired Bill since they had first met at Wheaton. For years, they had been on parallel tracks. Now their paths were converging, and they made plans to go to Ecuador as a team. Jim wanted to find a third man to go with them, and he did not know yet who that would be. When the team was complete, the three of them must learn four things: (1) Spanish and Quichua languages; (2) each other; (3) independence in jungle living; and (4) God's way to reach the jungle Quichua of Ecuador.[4]

When the linguistic course ended, Jim decided to remain in Oklahoma for a few weeks with Bill Cathers. They could spend the time learning to work as a team. They helped in the small assembly in Oklahoma City and in the Bible study group at the university. They advertised themselves as handymen in the local newspaper and made enough money painting and fixing things to sustain themselves while they carried out this ministry. Jim's life was made of many of the mundane things he had done while living in Portland. Only now he was one giant step closer to his goal.

Jim began his overseas travel plans by applying for

a passport. Dr. Tidmarsh wrote that he planned to take a furlough and urged Jim and Bill to come as soon as they could. They planned to visit their homes once more, gather essential supplies—"nothing like most married couples require," Jim commented—and raise the necessary funds for the voyage and support.

At the end of September, Jim received word that his oratory award-winning friend and fellow prankster, Ed McCully, had decided to quit law school and look for opportunities for missionary service. Perhaps Jim's locker room exhortation in 1949 had had an effect after all. Now Jim wondered if Ed would be the third man he was praying for. It seemed more than coincidence that Ed should suddenly be looking for missionary work at the same time that Jim was praying for a partner.

A few weeks later, Jim left Oklahoma—though he felt there was much work yet to be done—and traveled to Milwaukee to be with Ed McCully. He earned his keep there by painting the McCully family's home, all the while wrestling with the question of whether Ed would be the next member of the team bound for Ecuador. He shared his plans for Ecuador with Ed, including the possibility that Ed should join the team. Jim was conscious, though, that Ed had left law school to follow the leading of God, not to follow the leading of Jim Elliot. He wrote in his journal, "I sense crisis for Ed and the danger of influencing him wrongly, so grant me wisdom in all that I say among the family here."[5]

In fact, Jim felt that Ed's decision about Ecuador should not be made while Jim was with the McCully family. They influenced each other too easily; their friendship might override a sense of God's leading. Now that his own future was clear, the patience that Jim had cultivated for so many years was tested by waiting for an answer about whether Ed McCully would also go to Ecuador.

EIGHT

Ecuador was on the horizon at last. As they waited for their paperwork to come through, every day of preparation put Bill and Jim closer to departure. Suddenly, the planning came to a halt. In the fall of 1950, a letter came from Dr. Tidmarsh saying that he was going on furlough in England. Jim and Bill had counted on being introduced to the Quichua work under the tutelage of Dr. Tidmarsh. His years of experience would be a critical foundation to the work they could do. If Dr. Tidmarsh was not going to be in Ecuador, perhaps for as long as a year, they did not have to be in such a hurry. Jim and Bill could slow down their pace and prepare more thoroughly. Though perhaps disappointed at having to wait as much as a year, Jim had learned that God's timing would prove right in the end. He and Bill could put the months of waiting to good use building relationships with assemblies around the country.

Then the planning took another twist. Bill Cathers

decided to get married. Jim had been looking forward to going to Ecuador in a partnership with Bill. They knew each other well, worked together comfortably, and held similar convictions. Apparently, though, Bill no longer shared the conviction that he must go to the mission field as a single man. He still intended to go to Ecuador, but not single and perhaps not into the primitive work that Jim yearned for. Jim continued to believe that such mission work could best be carried out by young men unencumbered by wives and family. He himself had no inclinations toward marriage and doubted that he would ever fall for someone hard enough to want to be married, despite his long-distance involvement with Elisabeth. He described himself as a "bohemian loafer without enough sense of responsibility to get my shoes shined." [1] In other words, he was not marriage material.

From what Jim knew of missionary life, he had concluded that it would be hard to build relationships with the people he wanted to reach, learn the language and customs, and make a multitude of emotional adjustments. In his mind, it would be even more difficult for a woman. He had heard of too many cases where the wife was so absorbed in family responsibilities that she never had time to be a missionary. Jim held to his conviction that an unmarried man should go with another unmarried man. No matter what his feelings were for Elisabeth, and they were profound by this point, taking a wife as a missionary partner seemed unwise to him. The question now was, who would be his partner? Instead of anticipating the addition of a third member to the team, he was back to looking for one partner.

Jim finished painting the McCully house without

resolving the question of whether Ed would go to Ecuador. Then he moved on to his next opportunity, which was in Huntington, Indiana, a small town where a group of young married couples wanted to study the Bible. It was during these weeks that Jim became outspoken in his opinions about patterns of worship and church life. In his view, some of the young people felt bound up in traditional forms of worship and were fearful of breaking out of these forms. Though some accused him of unorthodox teaching, he maintained his view that the New Testament provided the pattern for worship and church life; organized denominations had strayed too far from the original pattern. However, he was aware of his limited time; unless someone else came to Huntington as a teacher and encourager in the New Testament pattern as he interpreted it, the group would not be able to carry on. This frustrated Jim. While unmarried people were needed for pioneer mission work in the Ecuadorian jungle, places like Huntington, Indiana, were perfect mission fields for couples and families. If only a married couple would stop dabbling with houses and babies and silverware and move in to a community like Huntington to teach the truth! Jim felt no connection with the stages that punctuated the lives of most American young adults. It was no secret that he considered such things as undesirable weights around the ankles of someone truly committed to God's service. In his mind, there were more important things to do.

After a few weeks in Huntington, Jim went with Ed McCully to another small town, Chester, Illinois. Their calling, as they saw it, was to evangelize, establish a Plymouth Brethren assembly, and gain experience in radio, medical, and educational work. All of these activities might have useful application to their future missionary work. Ed was now thinking seriously about going to Ecuador with Jim.

They embarked on sales jobs during the day and dedicated their evenings to various forms of outreach and ministry. Sharing a cramped apartment, they cooked together and memorized poetry. Beginning in January of 1951, on Fridays and Sundays they broadcast a radio program, taking turns preaching and announcing for each other. A male chorus from St. Louis contributed their music to the program, which was called "The March of Truth."

Ed and Jim also conducted services at the state prison and held Thursday evening meetings in a nearby town. They were invited to present an assembly in the local high school. Although they were billed as a program for "moral, religious, and uplifting purposes," their aim was to preach the truth of the resurrection of Jesus Christ. Despite their high hopes, they were disappointed at the outcome. The message and music seemed not to hit the mark, making little impact on the students. Discouragement set in.

In his journal, Jim recorded: "Was much cast down in spirit last evening. Ed and I have been here in Chester six weeks and with so little evident blessing from God that the questions which plagued the psalmist have come to us persistently: 'Where is thy God?' and 'Who will show us any good?' "[2]

After six weeks, they had seen no conversions except for one salesman who was from out of town. In spite of their ambitious beginnings, they seemed to be making little impact on the community of Chester itself.

Some would consider that six weeks, or even six months, was a very brief period of time on which to judge a ministry's effectiveness. After all, they had come to Chester completely unknown to the town and with no outside support for the tasks they took on. This is a difficult beginning for any project. For Jim that was no excuse. He was eager for results.

Nevertheless, they continued. A wealthy widow eventually gave them permission to use a vacant store she owned to begin a Sunday school, and they were grateful to have a regular place to carry out their work. They launched the Sunday school on March 4, with seventeen children attending. By Easter, they had forty-three children attending.

As he worked closely with Ed, Jim continued to wonder if Ed might be his partner for Ecuador.

But on April 28, his hopes were dashed. Ed purchased a diamond ring and became officially engaged a few days later. Though Ed was still committed to going to Ecuador after he got married, he would not be the single partner that Jim was looking for. He also wanted further preparation before he would go to Ecuador, and so would not go to the field as soon as Jim hoped to go.

First Bill, now Ed. It was hard for Jim to see the college gang breaking up as they married off, while he was left alone with his conviction that God meant for him to be single at this point in his life. During college they had all been single and visionary. Now Jim was the only one holding out against the pressure to conform. No doubt there were some, including Jim's own mother, who thought he should get down to business and make a commitment to Elisabeth. They were so alike in what they wanted that it seemed like an inevitable match. Dave, Bill, and Ed, Jim's three close friends, all chose to marry and continue in mission work. What held Jim back from doing the same?

During their last month of working together in Chester, Ed and Jim conducted tent meetings. While crowds were smaller than they had hoped for, they did see a number of conversions. Reflecting on their overall effort in Chester, Jim wrote: "Impossible to register the good God has done in Chester. I can see several reasons for coming now that I did not see in January. Surely the Lord has led. Still nothing 'big' or extraordinary in the work of the Gospel, and this I judge to be only because I lacked intensity and perseverance in prayer."[3]

In June 1951 Ed and Marilou got married. They intended to complete a year of basic medical training at a school in southern California. Bill Cathers married Irene the same summer. Jim was left floundering once more. He returned to Portland, arriving with $1.20 left in his pocket. He stayed a few weeks, engaging in manual labor and hours of reflections, as he had done the year before. Except that he now knew he could go to Ecuador, in some ways Jim was not any closer to the mission field than he had been a year earlier. For every two steps forward, his plans had taken at least one step back.

While Jim was home in Portland, the Tidmarsh family visited. Their visit made him more convinced than ever that he should go to Ecuador. He set a tentative sailing date of December 1, but first he wanted to take a trip east.[4]

It had now been more than a year since Jim's decision

to go to Ecuador. Understandably, he was ready to put the lengthy preparation process behind him and begin the true missionary phase of his life. But he had to be sure he had a partner. Before he left the Northwest for his speaking tour of assemblies in the East, Jim dropped in on a friend in Seattle, Pete Fleming. Pete was also part of a Brethren assembly, and the Fleming and Elliot families had been good friends. This particular mid-July visit, however, was not simply a chance for old friends to catch up. Jim had a specific purpose. He took Pete out for the afternoon, and they conversed for hours.

That evening, Jim spoke in Pete's assembly, sharing his call to go to the mission field as a single man and his need for a partner, so that he could follow the New Testament pattern, as he interpreted it, of carrying the gospel to other lands in pairs. Pete Fleming was impressed with what Jim had to say. At a crossroads in his own life as far as preparing for future ministry, Pete was heavily influenced by Jim's obvious convictions. Within a few weeks, Pete had abandoned plans to go to seminary and committed to going to Ecuador with Jim Elliot.[5]

One price to be paid for this decision was Pete's relationship with a young college student named Olive. They had dated for several years and were on the verge of engagement by the summer of 1951. But Jim Elliot's visit changed the course of their relationship. Pete was now convinced that he should go to Ecuador with Jim and that he should remain single, at least for a while. What the future held for him and Olive, he did not know. As if taking his cues from Jim's relationship with Elisabeth, Pete put everything on hold, assuring Olive that he loved her but making no commitment for the future.

Jim set off across the country once more, traveling with Pete to give talks in the New York area. They were making the rounds speaking in churches that might support them in their work in Ecuador. Bill Cathers was with them as well.

Jim saw Elisabeth again during this trip, for the first time in over a year. They managed to squeeze in a picnic in the New Jersey pines, lunch in Philadelphia, and a day in New York. As they talked, Jim hinted that it might be possible that God intended them to be together someday. Elisabeth waited for news that the red light had turned green. But it had not. Jim wrote in his journal, "Nearer to her now than ever, yet more confident that God is leading me away from her, to Ecuador with Pete, and she to the South Seas! This is a strange pattern."[6]

When the speaking tour was over, Elisabeth's brother Phil and his wife accompanied Jim, Pete, and Elisabeth to the Howard family vacation home in New Hampshire. They hiked the mountains and soaked up the beauty around them. One day, they took a trail that was interwoven with a rushing mountain stream. Jim paused to point out to Elisabeth that the water was separated into two streams in more than one place, but at the end of the trail it came together in a deep, calm pool. It was an allegory for their relationship, he said, and it gave her hope to keep hoping.

New emotions were stirring in Jim, as he recorded in his journal. "I am discovering Betty all over again these days. She has taken on a new meaning and power—and purity. Last two nights on top of Shelton delightful. Her body, once the thing that disturbed my thoughts of marrying her, seems now to fit the picture well. Thank God for her! Pure and warm and relaxed in my arms—I never guessed it could be. Waiting will be a trial, but loving her purifies me, somehow."[7]

And later, "I cried a little at thoughts of leaving her."[8]

And then, "She smiled after tears and prayer and told me she loved me."[9]

At the end of October, Jim visited the Howard home in New Jersey for a day or two of rest. Jim and Elisabeth posed for their first photograph together and then drove the twelve miles to the railroad station, where they separated yet again without a commitment for the future.

In the next few weeks, several circumstances in Elisabeth's life changed and seemed to point her future away from Africa or the South Seas and toward Ecuador. Jim and Elisabeth were aware that onlookers might be doubtful of the validity of her decision to go to Ecuador; it might appear that she was chasing Jim, since that was clearly where he was headed. But between them, they knew better. If they both ended up in Ecuador, it would be because God had taken them there separately. Jim still felt that he should begin jungle missionary work as a single man. Until he knew what that rough life would require of him, he would not know whether he could make a commitment to a woman that he would be able to fulfill.

Back in Portland, Jim began gathering supplies. By this time, Pete Fleming had confirmed his plans to go to Ecuador with Jim. Although they missed their December 1 sailing date, it seemed reasonable that they would be able to leave in February of 1952.

Jim continued to think of Elisabeth in a serious way. In late November, he wrote, "I began last night to consider engagement with Betty. Frightens me to think of finally leaping over all the old barriers I've raised against marriage. I feel strongly that for my own stability, for Betty's ease, and for most folks' tongues, I should buy a ring."[10]

Even this tentative decision caused a problem internally for Jim. "What shall I say to all the liberty I've been given to preach adherence to Pauline method—even to single men working on the field and illustrating it from Pete's intention and my own? What will men think who have heard me say, 'I go single, in the will of God,' when, if I were really engaged, my plans would be otherwise."[11]

But two days later, his thoughts had settled into a more familiar pattern: "I feel now as though it may mean five years of single life yet. Then, maybe after I'm thirty, getting paunchy, wrinkling and balding even, then the marriage bed!"[12]

Jim did not buy an engagement ring.

On February 2, 1952, late at night, Jim telephoned Elisabeth from San Pedro, California. He was en route to Ecuador. This was the first time they had spoken on the telephone. He told her he loved her, and asked, "Do you love me?"

To which she replied, "I can hardly help myself."[13]

He sailed the next day for Ecuador.

NINE

Heat and humidity nearly smothered them, blasting into their faces to make sure they knew they were in a new place. Pete and Jim had finally set foot on Ecuadorian soil on February 21, 1952. They had been at sea for eighteen days by the time they arrived at Guayaquil, Ecuador.

While on ship, they had had their first experience of cultural adjustment. On the first evening on the ship, they had dressed casually for dinner and discovered that all the other passengers were dressed quite formally. So they had worn coats and ties to breakfast the next morning and found everyone else wearing casual clothes. Obviously, they could not plunge into a new situation using the same assumptions by which they had lived their whole lives. The rules were different on the ship, and they would be still more different in a new country. They had a lot to learn. Fortunately, Dr. Tidmarsh would be their guide when they finally reached Quichua territory.

They got off the ship and were absorbed into their surroundings—a sea of faces in all directions and store windows hawking a surprising array of goods from sweaters and typewriters to fake shrunken Indian heads. To everyone around them, it was an ordinary day. For Jim and Pete, it was like no other day they had ever lived. The day called them to a future with a host of unanswered questions and challenges they had not yet imagined.

The immediate challenge was to figure out where they were supposed to go after getting off the ship. They had expected Dr. Tidmarsh to meet them, but he was not there, and they had no way to communicate with him. Using the smattering of Spanish that Jim knew, they found their way to a hotel on their own and tried to sleep in a room infested with mosquitoes. They slept little that first night. Three days later, Jim wrote to Elisabeth, describing the heat and mosquitoes as treacherous. He had heard the town clock every fifteen minutes most of the night and was still scratching three days later.[1] Not exactly the grand beginning he had imagined.

The next morning, their perspective brightened. Dr. Tidmarsh arrived at last, and they indulged in lengthy discussions about the work that lay ahead of them. While they waited for their belongings to arrive and clear customs, they soaked up the culture around them in Guayaquil: people stirring cocoa beans with their bare feet on the pavement, a boy with a monkey on his head, bargaining with a local merchant to reduce the price of an item by half.

Pete and Jim soon left Guayaquil and flew to Quito. Jim wrote of his experiences to his family. The city, old and picturesque, was situated between two mountain ranges.

On the west side, an active volcano had let off smoke within the last few days. Despite the volcano, the mountain was cultivated nearly to the top. In the city market, Jim could see the contrast that characterized Quito: an aristocrat in a fur coat shopping beside a beggar in rags.[2]

But Jim had not come to Quito to savor cultural contrasts. Quito was only a stepping stone, a place for further preparation. His primary objective there was to learn Spanish so he could function independently enough to move on to Shandia and the work that Dr. Tidmarsh had left.

In the first weeks in Quito, Jim struck up an important friendship—with a young man named Abdón who was willing to help Jim learn Spanish along with the formal instruction he was taking. Of course, Jim also hoped to share the good news of Jesus with Abdón, and it was in the course of this relationship that he came to realize that, in the long term, his real work would be to train Ecuadorians. Only Ecuadorians would be able to reach their own people and present the gospel. Whatever Jim did would only be a beginning, a link to the real work. He had to look for ways to help Ecuadorian Christians share the truth with their fellow countrymen.

In Quito, the two young men met with their friends Bill and Irene Cathers, Dr. Tidmarsh's wife and son, and another missionary named Dee Short. They needed an orientation to the mission work of the Brethren in Ecuador. And they had to learn Spanish as quickly as they could.

People plunged into a new culture often have fluctuating emotions, and Jim was no exception. Coming face to face with what he had committed himself to was overwhelming at times. His emotions went up and down during this period of adjustment. On March 2 he wrote, "Don't feel that I'm getting anywhere, either in the Word or in Spanish. Went to the street with T. (Tidmarsh) yesterday morning; longed to be able to preach."[3] His words reflected his frustrations and discouragement. But a few days later, he was able to write, "This marks the end of my second week in Ecuador. God has been faithful. Enumerating answered prayer is something I have not often done, but it is fitting tonight."[4]

Jim later left Quito for Santo Domingo where Dee and Marie Short were working with the Colorado Indians. Here he faced the mundane realities that often make up missionary work. "March 17. Living with Short these days and trying to be of some help around as well as sizing up the work and keeping Spanish before me. Most of the time it amounts to plenty of little things—washing dishes, helping with the kids, playing the harmonica in the open air, helping drive the truck. Yesterday we had a good meeting in the room off the plaza; lots of interested men."[5]

From there, Jim rode a horse down a road that was impassable for any vehicle, full of mud and holes. After a four-hour ride, he arrived in San Miguel to see the work of two women missionaries, Doreen Clifford and Barbara Edwards. They were considering beginning a school among the Colorado Indians. Then, having completed his introductory survey of the Brethren work, he returned to Quito and began a short course in practical medicine that he would need to put to use in the jungle.

After only two months in Ecuador, during which time surely no one expected Jim to be fluent in Spanish, he was frustrated at his lack of progress. The biggest obstacle, in his view, was that he had not been able to find an Ecuadorian home to live in. He and Pete had been staying at the Gospel Missionary Union compound where they were surrounded by people who spoke English. What they needed was to be surrounded by people who spoke Spanish and no English. They needed to be forced to use the Spanish they had already learned and pushed to learn more from their immediate context. Eventually, they were able to move into the home of an Ecuadorian family with five children. Progress in Spanish improved rapidly after that.

As April arrived, Jim anticipated the arrival of Elisabeth. Although she had been headed for Africa, that opportunity had not materialized; instead, she had come to believe she should go to Ecuador. They were both aware of what people might think. "April 6. Betty should be in Ecuador a week from tonight, God willing. Strange that we are led so close together so soon—wonderfully strange! There will be talk, especially at home, but I tend not to care a bit for it here. Let them talk, and God shall lead us on!"[6]

When she arrived, he recorded a poem in his journal:

> She came today;
> Stepped off an airplane
> And watched her feet walk down the steps;
> Looked up at friends
> And frowned a little.
> The sun was brighter than the plane,
> That made her frown;
> That, and the not seeing me
> Among the friends.

94

She hesitated
Wondering which side the fence
To walk up toward the building
Where I was waiting,
Watching her. And then
She saw me;
Came straight on,
Stepped up and stood
Before me, wondering
What I would do.
I took her hand, smiled
And said,
"Sure good to see you."
So it was, and so it is
Now that she has come. [7]

It was four days before Jim and Elisabeth had a private moment together. Jim had prayed for a chance to be alone with her, and finally the time came. He took advantage of the opportunity to embrace her and ask her if she was happy. Her answer displayed how hard the waiting had become for her; waiting in love, indefinitely, with no commitment from Jim that their relationship would not be suddenly cut off. This must have been hard for Jim to hear, knowing that he could offer no easy answers.

An obvious possibility was engagement. Jim was delighted to have Elisabeth in Ecuador. This was the first time since college days that they had been in close proximity to each other on a daily basis. It seemed clear that the Lord had led them one step further down the path—they were both in Ecuador at the same time, instead of in missionary service on separate continents. Yet Jim could not say for certain that the time for engagement had come, or when it might come.

From Elisabeth's perspective, he seemed inconsistent. He could speak quite plainly about marriage to her on the one hand, yet on the other hand, be so unsure whether it would ever happen. But Jim maintained his conviction that as long as he could be more effective in reaching a primitive tribe as a single man, then he would stay single. That could be years more. He could make no promises.

In the meantime, Jim and Elisabeth made the most of being together. Elisabeth and her companion found a room with a family just across the street from where Jim and Pete were living. The four of them threw themselves into language study as their first priority. The sooner they learned Spanish, the sooner they could move on to jungle work. Spanish pervaded the entire day. The foursome even ate their midday meal together, during which time their host stretched their Spanish ability.

Jim and Elisabeth took long walks, as they had during other phases of their relationship. They explored every corner of Quito, seeing the outdoor markets, museums, and craft shops. Together, they rode the bus in the afternoon to pick up the mail at the post office.

In June Jim leaped at an opportunity to make an aerial trip over the eastern jungle, the area in which he eventually hoped to live and work. This was his first chance to look for some evidence of where the Aucas were settled. Jim and other missionaries had heard that the Quichuas in the eastern jungle had had some friendly contact with the Aucas, who were known for their brutal treatment of outsiders. The information proved to be false. In fact, the truth was that the Aucas had recently killed five Quichuas in that area.

Jim did not find the Aucas on that trip. He was aware that the Auca population may have been only a few hundred. Statistically, they were an insignificant number of people, especially when measured against the millions of Ecuador and all of South America. Still, they were untouched with the Gospel, and Jim wanted to reach them. He returned to Quito more enthusiastic than ever about eventually reaching the Aucas.

Jim and Elisabeth had four months together with the daily contact that they had lacked for nearly four years. During this time, he knew that the Lord had brought Elisabeth and him over some happy ground. They had not asked to go to the same country, or to live across the street from each other. In fact, they had not even asked God for a relationship with each other. Yet there they were, living close together and seeing each other every day. In Jim's view, letting God lead was far better than pressing for his own dreams.[8]

TEN

Despite the ambiguity between them, Jim and Elisabeth took full advantage of their time together in Quito to enrich their relationship. They climbed the surrounding mountains more than once. On one occasion, they left their rooms at two in the morning with friends to view the area around Quito by moonlight, then had breakfast at 13,000 feet before climbing to 15,500, one of the highest spots on the mountain. On the way home, they let themselves separate from the rest of the group for a few minutes alone.

When their language teacher was ill for several days and they could not take classes, Jim welcomed the extra leisure time with Elisabeth. When a rain storm sent them running to a goatshed for shelter, they immersed themselves in a lengthy discussion of women in New Testament missionary work. It was easy to spend most of a day climbing a mountain and wandering around the rim of a crater.

Dr. Tidmarsh, eager for Jim to be ready to go to

Shandia, let them know what he thought about their excursions. He was not pleased. After all, climbing mountains in the moonlight had little to do with Jim's preparation for Shandia or Elisabeth's readiness for wherever she might go. Indulging in such outings surely was a distraction, in his mind. Jim was not bothered by Dr. Tidmarsh's remarks—they always took an Ecuadorian along with them on long outings for language work, so it was not wasted time.

Not every moment together was sweet. For instance, on one occasion, Jim hurt Elisabeth by making her feel that she was not free to make plans for activities that did not include him. "She didn't say good-bye with her eyes as she usually does," he wrote despondently in his journal shortly after the incident. [1]

But such brushes were the exception rather than the rule. In general, the months in Quito were overwhelmingly satisfying. Jim's journals during those weeks contain far fewer reflections on Bible passages and more contemplations of the love that had sprung up between them and endured for four years. Jim even wondered if it was right for him to be so happy.

On May 4 of that spring, Jim wrote, "Couldn't keep my eyes off of Betty. She is attractive in so many ways." But the next day, he wrote, "Marriage is not for me now; it simply is not the time. I do not say, and never did say, 'It is not the thing for me.'" Many years later, Jim's friend David Howard chuckled at this journal entry; his memory of Jim's statements during college about being a eunuch for the Kingdom was that Jim was quite firm on this point. Apparently Jim's feelings for Elisabeth had softened his perspective somewhat. In any event, he finished his

May 5 journal entry with, "With tribes unreached which I now believe reachable only by unattached me, 'I will not do this thing.'"[2]

By August, Jim had been in Quito for six months, and his Spanish was quite good. In fact, some Ecuadorians commented on his excellent pronunciation and found it difficult to believe he had learned Spanish so well in such a short time. He was ready to move on to the next phase, Quichua work.

Elisabeth's future was not clear, although she would go to an assignment with her partner. Jim and Pete, however, still aimed to help Dr. Tidmarsh and the work at Shandia. The time came for Jim and Elisabeth to part. Once again they had come to no specific commitment about the future of their relationship. They did not know when they would see each other again. Although they were in the same country, nothing was certain. They agreed that they should not make any public announcement about their relationship; in fact, they remained "undeclared" to one another, although their feelings for each other were undeniable.

Jim and Pete first went to a mission station known as Shell Mera to help with a boys' camp. They took eighteen boys with them from Quito. After the camp, it was on to Shandia, the station where the Tidmarshes so badly needed help. Because of his wife's health problems, Dr. Tidmarsh had had to abandon the work in Shandia. With Jim and Pete, he shared the hope that they would be able to reopen the work and, in fact, expand it. Their task would be to reopen a boys' school that had operated previously, to repair run-down buildings, and to add new buildings to accommodate future growth of mission work at Shandia.

Situated in the middle of the jungle, Shandia could be reached only by air, courtesy of a Missionary Aviation Fellowship plane. Since Shandia did not have its own airstrip —it had long ago been reclaimed by the jungle—the men were let down on the nearest airstrip, Pano, and then had to hike through the jungle to Shandia. Normally, this was a three-hour excursion. But Jim, who arrived a day after Pete, landed late in the afternoon and had to race against the darkness that would soon overtake the tropical area. He slid through the mud, stumbled over fallen branches, and ducked under low-hanging limbs. He finally reached the Shandia station just as the moon rose.

Curious Indians immediately surrounded the newcomers. Some of them looked familiar to Pete and Jim from photographs Dr. Tidmarsh had sent them. They understood little of what went on around them. Having barely mastered Spanish, they were now plunged into the Quichua language and faced the monumental task of learning it as rapidly as possible—without the aid of formal textbooks and study programs that had helped them with Spanish. Dr. Tidmarsh could visit periodically for a week or ten days at a time, but he could not stay long in Shandia after escorting them there. As soon as Jim and Pete were on their feet in the work, he would rejoin his family, and the young men would be on their own with everything, including the language. During those first weeks, Pete and Jim became familiar with the slimy route through the jungle. All of their gear was flown into Pano and had to be carried to Shandia on the backs of Indians looking to earn some money.

Shandia was high on a cliff above the Atun Yaku

River, the "big water" in Quichua language. Nearby, the small Shandia River ran into the bigger Napo River, which flowed down from the snowcaps of the mountains. Jungle living was rugged. Taking a bath meant going down fifty-five steps to the river. Pete and Jim employed about forty men to clear the jungle for an airstrip.

While the Quichuas worked outside, Jim and Pete studied language in the house. The house was a basic structure with a board floor and bamboo walls, bamboo ceiling, and heavy paper on top to keep out bat droppings. The men could look out long, screened windows to the river, the airstrip, and the ball field, and from another part of the house, out to the garden and the uncleared forest fifty feet away. [3]

Life was indeed rustic and isolated. The wild jungle around them cut them off from the civilization of Quito. Without their own airstrip, they could not even make easy contact with other mission stations. They were limited to a two-way radio. Mail was literally at a mule's pace, since it was taken out of the jungle on the backs of mules. Nevertheless, Jim was full of satisfaction at having reached Shandia at last. For the first time, he felt like a full-fledged missionary.

Jim and Pete, although welcomed by the Indians, were less than welcomed by the local Catholic priest. When it had appeared that no Protestant missionaries would take over the work of Dr. Tidmarsh, the local Catholics had been ready to pounce on the opportunity. So when Jim and Pete arrived, dashing the hopes of the priest, the two groups got off to a rough start.

On one of their first Sundays in Shandia, Jim and Pete joined more than fifty Indians in the home of

Venancio, one of the Indians who worked for them. Venancio had taken the young men under his wing and treated them as his sons. They had gathered for singing and gospel teaching despite the effort the priest had made the day before to get the Indians to attend mass on Sunday morning. When the priest discovered where they were gathered, he blundered into the group, refused Pete and Jim's gestures of friendship and cooperation, and reprimanded the Indians for not being in mass. His tirade over, he stalked out the door. He clearly saw Jim and Pete as a threat to his own effort and was especially concerned that they would try to lure his students away from his school to theirs. The Quichuas were caught in the middle. They understood little of the centuries-old tension between Catholics and Protestants. Yet they were being asked to choose between two things that probably seemed equally good to them.

Pete and Jim learned some lessons from the irritated priest, who seemed to them to be out of touch with the needs of the Quichuas. Witnessing his attitude of superiority made them work even harder to understand the Quichua language and to make room in their lives and schedules for as much contact with the Quichuas as possible.

They could not avoid major cultural confrontations, nor did they want to. Eagerly they shared everything from the colorful joy of a Quichua wedding to a traditional pig feast. They did not wince at things that might have horrified many North Americans.

Pete and Jim studied Venancio as a typical Quichua. Venancio walked the jungle trails in his bare feet. Shoes would have been ludicrous when his feet sank into the

103

mud, sometimes up to his knees. He carried his machete everywhere to clear his path as he walked. His wife trudged along behind with their baby strapped to her side and a large basket of food and household items strapped to her forehead. She also carried her machete, ready to dig manioc roots at any time. It did not take long before Pete and Jim realized how indispensable the machete was to life in the jungle.

A typical day began when they contacted the MAF Shell Mera station and other regional stations with radio. Then, they usually ate breakfast and started the workmen on various projects. The airstrip was the first priority. After radio contact again in the early afternoon, they would frequently take trips to nearby settlements to tend to the physical needs of the Quichuas. Though neither of them was a doctor, Jim and Pete had to learn quickly about practical remedies to problems common in the jungle. Dr. Tidmarsh—who was a doctor of philosophy and not a medical doctor—had years of experience to draw on. Pete and Jim accompanied him as he administered rudimentary medical treatment.

Their excursions consisted of treks into the jungle as well as riding in dugout canoes. A limited supply of drugs and caring hearts were all they had to offer. This motivated them to learn to do things most people never do. One of the first things they had to learn was to give injections, which Jim learned to do before Pete.

Living in a jungle culture also meant they had to eat things most people would never eat. On September 24, 1952, Jim Elliot ate his first ant.

A few days later, September 30, an even more significant event occurred. The airstrip was finally complete.

Jim and Pete were on the radio most of the morning covering the first flight to Shandia. More than 150 Indians gathered to watch as the Piper Cub landed with its load of bread, meat, vegetables, sugar, and lentils. Elisabeth had known about the flight and sent a birthday package for Jim—honey, peanut butter, candy, and Ritz crackers. This connection to the region around them, Pete and Jim believed, would advance their work rapidly, as well as encourage their spirits and nourish their bodies with needed supplies. No longer would they have to trek back and forth to Pano to get what they needed.

In the midst of all the work and primitive conditions, Jim took time to appreciate the beauty of the creation around him. He wrote to Elisabeth about his surroundings. The birds' songs in the forest enchanted him with their long, low whistles, canary-like tunes, or mellow hoots. At night, the bird sounds were less frequent and overshadowed by the racket of crickets and other insects. The sounds were so fantastic that Jim considered recording the night sounds for others to hear, from the squeaking bats in the thatched roof to the thundering rapids below the cliff.

Gradually, Jim and Pete learned the Quichua language. They carried little notebooks everywhere. Quichua was an unwritten language. They did not have the advantage of being able to look at a word on a page, much less pronounce it and try to use it. Instead, they had to listen carefully and discern the sounds on their own. They would write down what they heard, or what they thought they heard, and then go about trying to figure out what that particular pattern of sounds meant.

Superstition abounded. When missionary efforts at

medical treatment seemed to fail—or when they could offer no appropriate treatment—the Quichuas would resort to calling in the witch doctor, who would perform rituals and traditional cures that had little effect against illness and death. When this happened, Jim and Pete faced the greatest challenge of their work with the Quichuas. Could the news of the New Testament free the Indians from their fear and superstition? If they knew the Bible, would the Quichuas also know freedom from fear of death and evil spirits?

Convinced that the Quichuas themselves must learn the Scriptures so they could teach their own people, Jim and Pete threw themselves into reopening the school that Dr. Tidmarsh had been forced to close. They taught the children to read and write, with the goal that some day they would read the Bible for themselves.

Jim's thoughts and prayers continued to extend beyond the Quichuas. The Aucas were never out of his thinking. At least the children in Shandia could hear Bible stories and learn about the love of God. But the Aucas had never heard any Bible stories or known about God's love. Realizing that their immediate work was with the Quichuas in Shandia, Pete and Jim also looked for the day when God would send them to the Aucas.

ELEVEN

J im looked up from his wash basin to greet the spectacular dawn breaking over the forest. Unblighted by signs of civilization, free of imposing buildings and blaring traffic, morning in the jungle was purely and simply beautiful. At Shandia, Jim had plenty of opportunities to reflect on the beauties of the creation around him.

On this particular morning, as he looked out to where the cliff hung over the river, Jim saw a young woman dumping some litter over the edge. She was discarding the evidence that she had given birth the previous night to a still-born baby.

"Made my first coffin this morning," Jim wrote to his parents later that day, his words belying the fact that he knew it would not be the only coffin he would make. He used pieces from the crates that the radio equipment had come in, discarded scraps now put to a precious use. The woman, who Jim thought would have been grieving, went about her task without emotion. Dr. Tidmarsh had attended the breech birth, but the family had resented his interference, leaving him helpless to do something that might have helped. So Jim made the coffin, and the father dug the grave. Jim came face to face with the truth that life was not very important in the jungle, especially the life of a baby who had never breathed. It was as if the baby was not even human, but just a mess to be cleaned up.[1]

Life was fragile in Shandia. Jim Elliot's correspondence with family and friends during those first months of work contains many other references to burying babies. Sometimes it was a baby that Jim or Pete had tended. On one occasion, they lent kerosene to a family to encourage them to sit up and watch the baby all night. Instead, everyone in the house went to sleep. They found the baby dead and sent for Jim and Pete. Of course, it was too late. The mother and grandmother started the traditional three-pitched wail of grief—an awful thing to have to work beside while Jim and Pete tried to resuscitate the baby, whose body was still warm. Kneeling on a dirt floor beside a sunken-eyed baby, they cried out to God for a miracle, to put life back in the small body, to show His power among these people. But the baby was dead.

Soon the wake began in earnest. The parents chanted their grief, while others embarked on playful laughter, an odd—to Jim—Quichua custom. Rather than console the family in their loss, the guests at the wake were expected to play and drink all night from a half-gourd to distract and entertain the grieving family.[2]

For years, Jim had concentrated on making himself physically and spiritually fit for pioneer missionary

work. And now here he was, in the throes of it, facing
relentless obstacles that he could do little about. He was
not trained as a medical doctor; many times he could
only guess at the best thing to do. Even in situations
where he knew what to do, Quichua superstitions and
traditions held him back. As in the case of the dying
baby, too often the Quichuas would wait until a medical
situation became a crisis before seeking the outside help
of the missionaries, and by then it would be too late.
What was minor or routine in the States, treated easily
with common drugs, always had the potential in the
jungle to be life threatening.

Had Jim's years of strategic preparation prepared him
for this? He knew his Bible forward and backward and
burned with a passion for preaching the gospel. He could
take a language apart and linguistically reconstruct it,
knowing that this process was key to reaching primitive
peoples. But could anything have prepared him for the
emotional toll of the hard life around him? Had any part
of his self-directed preparation readied him for the
fragility of life he now encountered every day?

In the face of these life-or-death demands on their
energy, it was difficult for Jim and Pete to make much
progress in the Quichua language. After three months
among the Quichuas they understood almost nothing.
Jim had memorized a few phrases that kept him from
getting over his head in a conversation, but in reality he
could not initiate and sustain any discussion. In Quito,
his task had been to focus on language and learn Spanish as quickly as possible. In Shandia, he did not have
that luxury. Language work was only one item on a long
list of tasks that had to be accomplished each day. Their

Jim ELLIOT

language time was constantly interrupted with crises that could not be ignored. It was not simply that they were busy with other projects, but that urgency was a way of life in the jungle.

For instance, on one occasion, Jim's study time was interrupted by Pete's shouting from the airstrip that a twelve-year-old girl had been bitten by a snake. Jim scrambled to do what he could to excise the poison from the girl's body. He stuck a clean blade on his scalpel and slit her skin to release the venom. Her cries of pain agitated onlookers, who thought he was hurting her. Jim knew the importance of drawing the venom out of the girl's body, but with his limited language he could not persuade the crowd that his actions, though causing pain, were necessary to save her life. He had to stop before he was sure that the job was done. He then tried to suction out the venom from the slits he had made, but the child screamed again. Jim had to settle for allowing her slow bleeding to cleanse the wound. Eventually, he left her, not knowing whether his actions had been successful. [3]

Interruptions could come from anywhere: a wrist in need of a splint, machete cuts, fevers, births, supervising the Quichuas who were working on construction projects, gardening so Jim and Pete would have enough vegetables to eat, motivating the school teacher, buying food, or a hundred other things. All this transpired while they swatted at insects in oppressive heat.

It was during a baby's wake that Jim first played a Quichua game—"Flip the Bowl." The players placed a bowl filled with a traditional dish on the floor. The first player then leaned over, grabbed the edge of the bowl with his teeth, and flipped it over his head. The objective was to do this without being drenched with the milky liquid the bowl contained. After watching several people do this with varying degrees of success, Jim stepped forward and performed perfectly on the very first attempt. This made quite an impression on the Quichuas.

In return, Jim and Pete introduced volleyball to the Quichua schoolboys, who also had learned to play soccer quite well.

Once the airstrip was operational, Jim and Pete concentrated on fixing up the old buildings, adding new ones, and improving the school. Despite their dedication, obstacles blocked their progress. By the first of October, while they were celebrating the victory of the airstrip and planning the general layout of the buildings, Pete battled diarrhea and vomiting. Watching his friend's pale face, Jim worried about him and wondered what he would do if his partner had to leave the jungle.

In November Jim wrote to Elisabeth that the work was going at a slow pace. Some of their students had dropped out, and their language study was interrupted constantly. Letters to family and friends that should have been written were not. Even visiting the Quichuas was not productive, at least in terms of evangelism, because they had learned only a smattering of Quichua. [4]

No matter how well laid their plans were, something always got in the way. Perhaps Jim felt that things were not going at a "ripping pace" because he was so eager to get on with evangelistic work. Some of the hurdles he faced originally may not have been part of his concept of mission work. Or perhaps focusing on the end goal of seeing lives changed by the power of Christ made him impatient with day-to-day realities. In any event, from time to time, he was discouraged, and understandably so.

It was not long before Jim had the answer to his question about Pete's health. Pete continued to have health difficulties on and off, and when they had been in the jungle for less than six months, he fell ill to malaria and had to be flown to Quito for several weeks of recuperation. This left Jim on his own at Shandia. Amid the hectic schedule, Jim had always been glad to have Pete with him to share the work. No doubt Pete's absence meant even more difficulty finding time to make headway with the language.

Without a mastery of the language, Jim could not really move toward his real goals. Without the constancy of good health, Pete's participation lagged. This was not exactly the missionary work that Jim had anticipated. Understandably, he found himself asking the same questions others might have asked: What kind of missionary work is this? Missionaries were supposed to leave their homelands to preach the gospel to unreached people all around the world. But Jim and Pete were running from one crisis to another. How was the gospel being preached by building coffins and throwing bowls of liquid over one's head? While he tried to suction that snake bite, Jim could not even communicate with the little girl to make her understand why he had to do things that caused her pain. But even in the midst of discouragement at the number of times his studies were interrupted or the dozens of things that always needed doing, Jim hung onto his belief that he had to understand the Quichuas in order to reach out to them. Staying up all night playing games after the death of a baby, while not his natural response, was what was appropriate to the Quichuas.

Without the benefit of long stretches of formal study, Jim and Pete had to absorb the Quichua language through the experiences which they shared with the people. The Quichuas had been surviving in the jungle for generations. Jim and Pete had much to learn if they were going to make it. They soon learned to swing a machete to make their way through the thick vegetation. Their diets were adjusted to what was available locally; bread was unheard of, so they ate manioc and plantain instead, or the strange, dark potato that grew on jungle vines. They visited homes, which were scattered here and there, with pencils in hand to record the nuances of sounds they heard.

When he did have time to work on language, Jim found it fascinating. He thought that the freshness of discovering a language from the speaker's mouth, without the aid of a textbook, was a stimulating challenge, rather than merely a frustration. He was especially interested in the tendency of the Quichua language to use words that mimicked sounds. For instance, a free-swinging broken wrist was described as going *"whi-lang, whi-lang."* The word had no substantial meaning that Jim could discern, yet it perfectly described the broken wrist. A flickering lamp went *"li-ping, li-pint, tiung, tiun."* The word *"tukluk, tukluk"* described rapid swallowing or gulping.[5]

As they were literally and figuratively carving a place for themselves in the jungle, Jim and Pete were also preparing the way for future missionaries at Shandia. Jim's college friend Ed McCully and his wife, Marilou, were still planning to come and join the work at Shandia.

Pete and Jim were eagerly looking forward to expanding the team. One of the new buildings they worked on was a house for the McCullys. First, of course, the McCullys had to spend a few months in Quito learning Spanish, just as Jim and Pete had done. Though the work had begun roughly with innumerable difficulties, the future loomed before them and they were eager to step into it.

TWELVE

The mountains rose majestically from the valleys, ruggedly slicing through the country. Snowcapped peaks glistened against the horizon, innocently cutting off east from west. The Andes mountains, at the center of Ecuador, now separated Jim Elliot from Elisabeth Howard.

Within a few weeks of Jim's departure from Quito to Shandia, Elisabeth headed off in the opposite direction. Her task, with her partner, was to analyze the language of a small tribe called the Colorados with the goal of reducing its complexities to a written form. The Colorados were in the western part of Ecuador; Shandia was in the eastern part. And two ranges of the Andes were in between. In addition to the challenges in their work, they had to adjust to infrequent and unreliable mail service for their communication, rather than the face-to-face contact they had enjoyed in Quito. Sending a letter and getting a response took six weeks.

The months with Elisabeth in Quito had left their mark on Jim. Only a few weeks after being separated, he wrote to Elisabeth that their time in Quito had put him on an entirely different emotional level. They had been separated before; in fact, they had spent most of their five-year relationship separated by thousands of miles. But this time was different for Jim. He missed her more keenly than he had during past separations and looked at their relationship in a new light.

When news reached Jim that Elisabeth would be going to work with the Colorados, he was strangely shocked. But why should he be surprised? She had come to Ecuador as a single missionary and was not tied to a commitment to Jim or anyone else. Following the pattern that Jim so heartily approved of, she had formed a partnership with another single woman. Then she'd completed her language work in Quito as efficiently as possible and offered herself for assignment where her gifts would meet the need. She had followed the same path that Jim had followed. Why should he now be surprised? Had the fact that Elisabeth had come to Ecuador rather than going to Africa unconsciously made Jim expect that she would be near him? Mentally, he knew that she was doing the right thing and going where God had sent her. But somehow he had not faced the reality that she would be sent off to some obscure place, far from him. Emotionally, he now had to come to terms with the reality that mail would be torturously slow and visits nearly impossible. Quito was at least accessible by plane now, and it was reasonable to think he might have reason to go there occasionally. But now, even if he did, Elisabeth would not be there. If he was to see her at all, he would have to put a lot of energy into planning and travel.

On the other hand, he was glad that Elisabeth was finally involved in some work that was worthy of her intellectual abilities. She had trained for her work as rigorously as he had, so he was glad that she, too, had reached her goal of missionary work with a primitive tribe and an unwritten language.

Although he did not yet reveal his intentions to Elisabeth, Jim thought seriously about engagement around this time. He went so far as to write to Ed McCully and ask him to buy an engagement ring. The Lord's leading of Elisabeth to Ecuador instead of Africa and the months they had enjoyed together in Quito made Jim ready to do something he could not do a year earlier. He had agonized about becoming engaged the previous fall, and in the end he had decided not to. Now, circumstances and his own sense of God's leading were different. He was ready for the next step.

However, in Jim's mind, engagement did not automatically mean they would set a date and plan a wedding. He had come to the point of believing that God wanted him to marry Elisabeth. This did not mean that he ought to do it soon. He did not take engagement lightly, and he did not consider it permission to rush ahead of God's direction. Engagement and marriage were distinct steps. And Jim was prepared for a long engagement. He still had a lot of work to do in Shandia before he could consider taking a bride.

During the Christmas holidays, many missionaries managed to gather in the capital city. To Elisabeth's dismay, Jim did not make it to Quito for Christmas in 1952. She had thought that if they were going to see each other at all, it would be on a holiday occasion. But it was not to be.

A few weeks later, she roused to the galloping of a horse, answered the knock on her door, and accepted a telegram that told her Jim was waiting for her in Quito. Now, for Elisabeth to get to Quito was no easy thing. She was working in a remote area; getting to Quito involved more than simply making radio contact to request a flight. Undaunted by the difficulties, Elisabeth packed a few things, climbed on a horse, and started the journey to Santo Domingo. After spending a night there, she rode in a banana truck for ten grueling hours to get to Quito. Once there, she had to endure a reunion with Jim in the presence of other people; they had to restrain their emotions and portray their public image of being simply missionary colleagues.

But that evening they were alone together at last. They sat by the fire and Jim put a ring on Elisabeth's finger. Of course, those closest to them, such as Pete Fleming, had known about their relationship. But an engagement would remove all doubt about their intentions toward each other. They were engaged. Now the world could know that they loved each other.

Their happiness came crashing down only a week later. Elisabeth had some routine X-rays taken and was quickly diagnosed as having tuberculosis in an advanced stage. She knew then that she could never marry Jim. He was called to jungle work and committed to spending his life in a rugged, demanding setting. Elisabeth would most likely recover from tuberculosis with the right care, but she could never live in the jungle and remain healthy. Never even considering asking Jim to live somewhere else, she expected that they would break their engagement.

Jim was not so easily dissuaded. They had waited five long years to take this step, and he had asked Elisabeth to marry him in the firm belief that this was what God wanted for them. At the very worst, the news about tuberculosis might mean that they would have yet another long wait before they could marry. He realized God might have in mind another change in circumstances that would allow them to be together at some point in the future. He wrote, "As for me, things are unchanged. She is the same woman I loved last night before I knew the tubercles were formed in her chest. If I had any plans, they are not changed. I will marry her in God's time, and it will be the very best for us, if it means waiting years. God has not led us this far to frustrate us or turn us back, and He knows all about how to handle T.B. . . .I don't know what it means. Only I know that God is in the generation of the righteous and guides their steps aright."[1]

Jim had to leave to go back to Shandia, leaving Elisabeth to face the medical treatments ahead of her. It could mean going to the States for three or four months of treatment, or it might mean life as an invalid.

One morning, back in Shandia, the radio crackled, and when Jim responded to receive the message, he was surprised to hear Elisabeth's voice. Rather than sounding despondent, she was incredulous with joy. "It was all a mistake," she said. There was no tuberculosis. In his journal, Jim speculated, "I wonder if God healed her in those ten days or simply proved our faith by a mistake. Whatever, He has done well, and I bless Him for her health."[2]

Jim made plans to visit Elisabeth again in the spring, this time in her own setting at San Miguel. They stood on the balcony of the creaking thatched-roof house that Elisabeth shared with her partner and talked about the house they might someday have in the eastern jungles. They still had no wedding date set. Jim had other buildings he had to complete at Shandia before he could build a home suitable for them to live in. Also, Jim was adamant that Elisabeth should learn the Quichua language before they could get married, and she needed some time to do that.

When her work with the Colorado language reached a point where it was possible to disengage, she turned over her language files and notebook to two other women working in San Miguel and moved to Dos Rios, a place that was only a six-hour walk from Shandia. After being separated by mountains and dependent on banana trucks for transportation, being only six hours from each other was an encouragement to them both. In Dos Rios, Elisabeth would learn Quichua as rapidly as she could. Neither Spanish nor Colorado were as urgent as Quichua was now. She lived with a missionary family already fluent in Quichua. She also talked avidly with Indians around her and attended church and Bible studies to immerse herself in the new language. Her aptitude for picking up languages was stretched once again—successfully.

Mail now depended on Indian carriers, but at least they did not have to wait six weeks for a response. In July Jim was able to visit her in Dos Rios. It seemed that, finally, their missionary work and their commitment to each other were coming together in time and place. In another few months, Shandia would be ready for Elisabeth, and she would be ready for Shandia.

Although the Tidmarshes had worked at Shandia in the past, when Jim and Pete arrived, it was as if they had to start over. The absence of the Tidmarshes, because of health, had left the station unattended. The buildings were inadequate, the school closed, and the airstrip overgrown. But their hard work was showing results. The airstrip and school were up and running, and the buildings were progressing on schedule. The McCullys were in Quito, preparing to come to Shandia. Pete Fleming had also become engaged to Olive in Seattle. She had recently undertaken the same rudimentary medical training in California that the McCullys had completed. The future of the work in Shandia looked bright: Three dedicated missionary couples would soon converge on the place, and several of them were conversant in Quichua. The team that Jim Elliot had dreamed of building for jungle work was coming together. Years of waiting and preparation would soon bear fruit. Consolidation of the Quichua work would mean that Jim Elliot was one step closer to reaching the unreachable Aucas.

THIRTEEN

The rainy season in the Ecuadorian jungle is not something to trifle with. Once the unrelenting rains set in, people living in the jungle must adapt their activities to this force of nature, fully surrendered to its inevitability.

The year 1953 was an especially torrential one. Some of the Quichuas insisted that the rainy season that year was the wettest they had seen in thirty years. Progress on Jim's construction projects under these conditions was sluggish and discouraging. Day after day, the workers were unable to build, or got less done than Jim had hoped. Jim and Pete were forced indoors and could only stand at the window and watch the water descend in thick sheets. Puddles formed in the clearing; then the puddles overflowed to become oozing mud. Before long, the land itself labored under the weight of the water it held. The soil could not absorb another drop of the insistent liquid.

The rains became more than an inconvenience;

they threatened the very existence of the Shandia mission station. As the Napo River rose to an alarming level and the cliff above began crumbling, Jim and Pete faced the reality that they had built too close to the water. If the river rose much more, some of the buildings would be in danger of sliding into its rushing currents. Jim was especially concerned about the McCullys' house, which had been under construction and was nearly finished. The simple fact was that the brand new house had to be dismantled and moved back about a hundred yards. Work crews had to redo work they had already done. Even having accepted this necessity, carrying out their plans was difficult. Working in the rain was next to impossible, but it had to be done.

One good thing that came from having to stay indoors for long stretches was the time Jim and Pete were able to spend on language study. They made more rapid progress than they had since they'd arrived. Still, it was a disappointment. Construction delays meant a major setback in the timetable that would allow the McCullys—and Elisabeth—to come to Shandia.

The rains continued unabated. The river swelled to its capacity, and still the rain came. For the second time in two months, Jim and Pete faced the possibility that the river would overflow and destroy their hard work. At the end of July, it rained for four days solid. On the fifth day, they knew there was no escape from the damage the rains would do.

They forced themselves to work on the Quichua dictionary in the morning, despite their anxiety about the weather. About noon, they could see from the house that the cliff had begun to break off, and the river surged toward their house. This time it was not a question of rethinking the location of the house and organizing a work crew. They had to act immediately. They had no choice but to abandon the house and get as much of their equipment out of it as possible. Storing their gear in the school, which was located farther from the water, Jim and Pete rapidly tore down the house they had been living in. The walls, the floor, the screening on the windows—everything had to come down. The lumber was too valuable to abandon to the swollen river. They must save what they could, and they had literally only hours in which to do it. Fortunately, the Indians helped.

Frantically, Pete and Jim threw their possessions into cans and boxes and shoved these into the arms of waiting Quichuas. They grabbed whatever was loose and sent it to dryer ground in an unbroken relay. Expecting to move to Shandia soon, the McCullys had already shipped eleven steel barrels filled with their household supplies to Shandia. Fortunately, the contents had not been unpacked. The barrels were now rolled through the forest to a safe place. Boxes of food, clothes, papers, and medical supplies were hauled away from the crumbling cliff. They used every container they could get their hands on. The river surged on, every hour closer to where they were working.

As Jim directed the crew where to put the pieces of the house, Pete started dismantling the medical clinic they had built. The clinic was the newest and best of the buildings; having to tear it down so soon after its construction was heart-wrenching. Yet there was no choice. If they did not, they would surely lose every bit of the materials they had invested in that building. That would be an enormous setback in funds as well as time. Pete and his crew pulled out cupboards, doors, floor timbers, and whatever they could pry loose.

They ran out of time. They had ripped up the inside of the house, and Jim was starting on the window screens when the front porch gave way and dropped into the river. Jim had to get out. Even the Indians, who had lived through many rainy seasons, began abandoning them to run to safer ground. Within a few minutes, what was left of the house pitched over the cliff. Jim and Pete watched it go, helpless to stop the heaving force that snatched away in a few moments nearly a year of hard work.

Still the rain came. Before long, Jim knew that even the school would not be safe. The hours of shuttling supplies and equipment from one place to another would have to be repeated. A few of the Indians—including their friend Venancio—remained with Jim and Pete. Somewhere along the way, Jim had lost his shoes in the mud. Now his feet were scathed and cut with every step he took. But he could not stop for his own comfort. Literally everything they had was at risk. For six long, wet, dark hours they lugged their equipment into the jungle. They lurched through the mud with staggering loads, not knowing how many trips they would be able to make before the river would claim the school as well.

Chunks of land and trees gave way to the thunderous power of the river as the men escaped to higher ground. They hardly dared look behind them to see what they were losing. Solid land, which had stood proudly above the river for eons, was no more. The surging water swept away any scrap of evidence of the work so carefully planned.

Exhausted and having done all they could, at three in the morning, Pete and Jim huddled in some blankets in the home of one of the Indians for a couple of hours of sleep. All too soon they heard Venancio shouting, and they raced back to the mission station to see that the school had gone while they had tried to sleep, along with the playing field where the school boys had played soccer and other games. The edge of the water was now only thirty feet from where they had stowed their equipment. Hardly able to believe this reality, they once again raced to lug equipment to safety. They had more help this time, and they cut a trail into the thick jungle to create a place where Venancio rapidly built a makeshift aluminum-roofed shelter. There they stored their possessions—what had not been carried off by thieving Indians—and hoped for the best.

At mid-morning, the river seemed to ease off, and further destruction seemed unlikely. Jim and Pete could now take stock of the situation more objectively. Enormous damage had been done. The McCullys' house, already moved back a hundred yards, now stood only thirteen feet from the edge of the cliff. Obviously it would have to be moved again. Five other buildings, the playfield, and a hundred meters of the airstrip were all gone. They had saved most of their equipment, but the barrel containing the McCullys' essential kitchen equipment was lost completely.

A year's worth of work had disappeared.

In Dos Rios, Elisabeth was standing by the radio. Her last contact with Jim had been two days earlier. She knew that the weather was threatening the Shandia station, but two days of silence had left her wondering exactly what had happened. She tried repeatedly to find out, but none of the regular Indian runners would risk the trip to Shandia for information; the river would be impassable, they believed, and not worth the risk. Finally, Elisabeth persuaded someone to go. Jim sent back a letter describing their condition. His simple summary was, "Shandia is no more." This was the raw truth. Nothing was left at the mission station to give any hope for going on. Jim wrote to Elisabeth from beside a fire, where he was trying to dry out and warm up. Their immediate plan was to get a tent set up and establish some semblance of housekeeping while they sorted out what to do next. Most of the equipment had been saved, but things were wet and jumbled up. Sorting things out would be a monumental task. Jim's mind tumbled with thoughts of what the disaster meant, both for the work at Shandia and his own plans to marry Elisabeth.

Renovating what remained seemed absurd—"stupid" was the word Jim used to describe the possibility of housing there. He and Pete could take temporary shelter in the homes of Indians, but it would be months before Shandia would be ready for a married couple with children, like the McCullys. And if the McCullys could not move to Shandia, what did that mean for Jim and Elisabeth's plans? What was already uncertain was now more so, if that was possible.[1]

When she received Jim's letter, Elisabeth left immediately for Shandia with a group of Indians. The discouraging task of seeing what was worth salvaging was already started, and she wanted to be part of it.

To make the situation more complicated, Jim had his first bout with malaria. Pete had fallen victim before, but Jim had resisted it until he'd had to spend thirty-six hours hauling gear in a torrential rain. In the midst of deciding what reconstruction to attempt, Jim was plagued with headaches, dizziness, and weakness that drove him to his bed. However, anything they did at Shandia at this point in time would be makeshift and temporary. The question had become whether they should reconstruct at all. Was the destruction of Shandia a sign that they should be looking at other places? Perhaps they had focused too much energy on Shandia. Before going on, Jim wanted to explore some other possibilities.

When Jim recovered from malaria, he and Pete and Ed made a survey trip of the area around Shandia. For twenty-one grueling days, the three of them hiked and canoed their way through the jungle. The heat was intense and the continuing rain thick for many of those days. Heavy vegetation hung out over the water, camouflaging wildlife and sometimes small houses. They visited the Quichuas they encountered along the way, estimating population in various places and evaluating likely sites for a new station.

The best spot, in Jim's opinion, was at the juncture of the Pastaza and Puyo Rivers, a place called Puyupungu. There, an Indian with fifteen children had begged the threesome to come and live among them and establish a school. Such an invitation was unheard of in Quichua territory, and the missionaries knew they should not gloss over it. If they were to choose an area where they had not been invited in, they would face the challenge of winning friendship and credibility. But if they accepted Atanasio's invitation, they could save valuable time and make much faster progress. Pete and Ed agreed with Jim that they should accept this invitation to go to Puyupungu.

Then the question was, who should go?

Ed and Marilou McCully had not yet learned Quichua. It would be months before they could adequately communicate in Puyupungu. If they took on the responsibility of beginning a new work from scratch, surely their language study would suffer. It made more sense to Ed that he and Marilou remain in Shandia, live in a simple house, and try to rebuild that station. They could do this if they also had the help of an unmarried man with some experience in carpentry and the language. Since Jim was already engaged to Elisabeth, and Pete was still unmarried, it seemed that the best arrangement was for Pete to stay in Shandia, at least until it was time for his own wedding. Jim and Elisabeth could be the couple who would begin the work in Puyupungu.

After the long years of waiting for direction in their relationship and prolonged uncertainty about when they could get married, suddenly the light was green. The need in the mission work was for a married couple who knew the Quichua language and had experience at a primitive mission station. Jim and Elisabeth fit the description—if they got married as soon as possible. So they did.

FOURTEEN

No church bells rang. No satin train trailed the bride. No delicate lace hid her face from her bridegroom. No reception beckoned family and friends to a grand celebration.

When the time came for Pete Fleming to get married, he planned to go back to Seattle for a full-scale church event that would include both his family and Olive's. But Jim and Elisabeth did not want that. They had agreed years ago that they were not interested in a conventional wedding with all the trimmings. Elisabeth enjoyed attending formal weddings but did not want one for herself. Jim was even more adamant that such weddings were vain and meaningless. Maturity had tempered him somewhat since college and the year or so after graduation, when he had seen several of his friends marry with traditional festivities, but his overall opinion had not changed.

So their wedding was a simple one, not even held in

a church. Jim wrote to his family of their plans only five days before the ceremony, clearly not allowing enough time for them to travel to Ecuador for the event. Instead of family members, the only "guests" at the wedding were the Tidmarshes, as official witnesses, and Ed and Marilou McCully. The whole thing was over in a civil ceremony that took less than ten minutes. They signed the legal register and were married.

Both were satisfied with the choice they had made. If they had taken time to return to the States, plan a church wedding, and go through all the traditional social stages of wedding and honeymoon, they would have been away from Ecuador for months. Neither of them wanted that. The time was ripe for going into Puyupungu; the choice was clear.

They did, however, take time for a brief honeymoon. First they went to Panama, and then on to Costa Rica, where they surprised Elisabeth's brother David and his wife, Phyllis, with their sudden news. Dave had not even yet heard that the marriage was imminent. He just opened his door one day and there stood his sister and his good friend, now husband and wife.

Then it was back to Quito to prepare for Puyupungu. Until this point in time, Jim had used very little of the original supplies he had brought with him from the States almost two years earlier. He had left a lot of his things stored in barrels in Quito. After the destruction and loss at Shandia, it seemed fortuitous that he now had access to fresh supplies. Elisabeth also had some supplies to contribute to their new start. Together, Jim and Elisabeth went through supplies that had been nearly untouched. Between the two of them, they had adequate supplies for setting up a household. The trek to Puyupungu began.

The farther they got from civilization, the more primitive their mode of transportation became. They packed their things in steel drums and flew to Shell Mera, where they stayed with Nate Saint, the Missionary Aviation Fellowship pilot, and his wife, Marj. But Nate could not fly them to Puyupungu, where there was no airstrip. Instead, Nate drove them down a narrowing dirt road that disappeared into the last town that was accessible by a land vehicle. This was as far as he could take them. From there, Jim and Elisabeth traveled by canoe to the village of Puyupungu, with Indian guides to transport them and their gear. As in Jim's early days at Shandia, Jim and Elisabeth were cut off from civilization. Only Puyupungu was even more cut off than Shandia. The job ahead of them was enormous, but for the first time, they were facing their work together, as partners.

When they climbed out of their canoe on the bank at Puyupungu, Atanasio greeted them. He was the man who had invited the missionaries to come and start a school. He now proudly escorted them on the last leg of their journey. His two wives and all his children came running down the beach, grabbed assorted boxes, drums, and other gear, and eagerly carried everything up the cliff. The coming of the missionaries was a cause for celebration.

With grateful eyes, Jim and Elisabeth saw the thatched house where Atanasio had arranged for them to live. It must have been a relief to see that they had immediate shelter after their grueling journey. But relief was short-lived, lasting not even a night. Unfortunately, the house was infested with cockroaches and the ceiling was so low that neither of them could stand up straight under the beams.

Fortunately, one of the last things someone had given Jim before he had left California to sail for Ecuador was a sixteen-foot square tent. On the morning after the first night in Puyupungu, he pitched the tent, and they moved in. He would build something more permanent as the work went along. For now, the tent was home, and they were grateful to have it.

Atanasio wanted a school for his children and other children of the village, and it was Jim and Elisabeth's job to provide one. They organized classes and found someone who could be a teacher under close supervision, although not to their complete satisfaction. In the meantime, they also began clearing an airstrip and working on a house. Puyupungu needed to be accessible by air and have at least one permanent structure available to missionaries if it was to be developed into a mission station. And this is what they intended. They had not come this far only to teach school to a handful of children. They wanted to establish a work that would eventually present Jesus to these Quichuas and prepare them to preach to their own people.[1]

Meanwhile, in Shandia, Pete Fleming and Ed and Marilou McCully were renovating the mission station. Most of the airstrip that Pete and Jim had cleared the year before was still useable, so Shandia was still accessible by air. Other than that, the work at Shandia, too, was starting over. Pete's experience from the previous renovation now bore fruit, and he was able to build more quickly and with better skill. While the Elliots were on their honeymoon and the McCullys were finishing their language preparation, Pete worked alone at Shandia and made tremendous progress. When he was ready for them—meaning that there was a place suitable for a family to live in—the McCullys moved to Shandia. Pete began preparing for his transition out of Shandia. He made plans to return to Seattle in June of 1954 to marry Olive, knowing that he would be gone for several months. Together, he and Olive would return to Ecuador and rejoin the work. Neither Pete nor Jim had lost sight of the goal of reaching the Aucas. As the mission stations among the Quichuas became more established, they would be able to devote some energy to the next frontier.

Jim and Elisabeth traveled to Shandia for Christmas with the McCullys and Pete Fleming. Right after Christmas, Pete, Jim, and Ed hosted a men's Bible conference. Forty Quichuas attended, crowding the small building in which they met. Jim and Pete had a good enough grasp of the language now that they could do solid teaching on the Bible in Quichua, something they had not been able to do before.

After the conference, they held a baptism service, something else that they had not done before in Shandia. Two Quichua girls were the first to be baptized. Afterward, several others approached Jim and Pete and said that they also believed and wanted to be baptized. After all of the setbacks that the work in Shandia had faced, at last there was some progress in the real work they had come to do. The tide had turned in Shandia. The missionaries had good reason to think that the work there would flourish from that point on.

Back in Puyupungu, things proceeded at a slower pace. Jim finished construction on their house, and he and Elisabeth were settled in it by late March. When Holy Week arrived that year, Jim took advantage of the custom of religious festivals and held nightly meetings, during which he preached on the seven last words of Christ. He felt that several people, including Atanasio, were close to understanding what it would mean to be a Christian.

Despite the fact that their house was just finished and they had barely moved in, Jim and Elisabeth's days in Puyupugu were numbered. Jim's father, always interested in the missionary work of his sons, had offered to come to Ecuador and help with building projects. This extra help came at a critical time. Pete, Ed, and Jim agreed that at least one of the mission stations they worked from should have permanent housing and be more fully developed. Other places, like Puyupungu, could serve as outstations until the time came that they could be developed more thoroughly. These places would serve as preaching points; the missionaries would stay in touch and minister in those places as much as they could, but not necessarily live there year-round. Eventually, Ed and Marilou McCully would set up a similar outstation in a place called Arajuno.

The time had come to put their plan into action. Ed and Pete wanted to take advantage of the presence of Jim's father to build up Shandia. It seemed logical that Jim should also be in Shandia to help. Feeling that the construction in Puyupungu was adequate for an outstation and since the school year had ended, Jim and Elisabeth moved back to Shandia in June of 1954.

They now lived in a small bamboo house that Pete had built. Jim put in long hard days of construction work, clearing land, hauling sand and rock, and supervising work crews. Working with Ed in the forest was a dream come true for Jim. Ever since their days together in Chester, Illinois, they had looked forward to being together in the jungle of Ecuador.

With the Elliots back in Shandia to work with the McCullys, Pete was free to leave for his wedding. He expected to be gone for about six months. He was committed to returning to the jungle—and the search for the Aucas—and Olive was committed to going where Pete went.

In addition to their construction work, Ed and Jim also went on preaching tours together, using Arajuno as a base as they had planned. They were encouraged by what they thought was genuine interest among the Quichuas in those areas. The highlight for them was that they were preaching the gospel to people who had never heard it before, unlike in Shandia, where Quichuas were more used to the presence of both Catholic and Protestant missionaries and perhaps did not take their message so seriously.

In Shandia the hopefulness that had come with the Christmastime Bible conference had waned. Though they'd had a good turnout for the special event, the week-to-week work was not nearly so encouraging. In fact, Jim was troubled by the lack of response in Shandia. Perhaps twenty-five Indians would attend a Sunday meeting, but almost all of them were school children. The few adults that attended were women. Jim felt it was imperative that he reach the Quichua men. He thought perhaps they had tired of his preaching. And perhaps his preaching was not what it should have been because of the distraction of ongoing construction work and the energy needed to sustain a marriage relationship. He tried to keep the steady ministry at Shandia in balance with the more exciting forays into untouched jungle areas.

Jim and Elisabeth spent their second Christmas at Shandia, this time alone. The McCullys had gone to Quito for the birth of their second child. Pete and Olive Fleming were also in Quito while Olive learned Spanish.

By February, everyone was back in Shandia and ready for another conference, similar to the one they had done the year before. This brought better results. They aimed at reaching and discipling young men. From seventy to a hundred people attended the sessions, and at the end, four young men were baptized. Jim was encouraged by this response because of his belief that the young men were the ones to carry the spiritual responsibility for the emerging church. With a nucleus of baptized believers to build on, Jim was able to give deeper instruction and to hold simple worship services during the week.

At first, Jim did most of the preaching, especially when Ed and Pete were away from Shandia. But he had long ago come to believe that the Quichuas themselves needed to take Christian teaching to their own people. To work toward this goal, he spent hours and hours going over portions of Scripture with a few young men on an individual basis. He taught them Bible study methods that they could begin to use on their own. Several of the young men showed talent for preaching, and Jim was eager to give them an opportunity. Soon they were able to take charge of the entire Sunday morning service.

Services, however, were trying times for other reasons. Jim and Elisabeth observed a major cultural difference in the Quichua approach to worship. As Americans, they were accustomed to people showing respect when the Word of God was read or preached, even if only outwardly. In a church in the U.S., people in the pew generally sit still and keep quiet during a church service. In the jungles of Ecuador, such behavior had never been learned. The women, in particular, were agitated, checking heads for lice or feet for thorns, or getting up to look at something that was going on outside the window. The men were not perfect, either; it was acceptable to stand up and talk to someone passing by the window while the service was going on. Dogs roamed the room while pet birds and monkeys perched comfortably on heads.

Under such distracting circumstances, Jim persisted patiently with building a church body at Shandia, always aiming at training leaders who would be ready to lead their own people.

In February of 1955, after the Bible conference, Jim and Elisabeth went to Shell Mera. Jim worked on a hospital construction project, and Elisabeth was soon occupied with their new baby daughter, born two days after their arrival in the home of Marj and Nate Saint. Jim immediately was enamored with his daughter, whom he named Valerie, although he and Elisabeth had not actually agreed on that name.

Nate and Marj Saint had a new baby in their house, too—a boy. The McCullys, still living in Shandia, now had two children. Pete Fleming had brought his bride back to Ecuador. Missionaries who had come to the field single or newly married were building families and showing their intentions for permanent residency in the Ecuadorian jungle. Fulfilling their calling to serve God did not, after all, mean denying themselves the love and support of a family. And their commitment to living in the jungle, even with small children, proved they were serious about that calling.

FIFTEEN

Perfect strangers can become fast friends within a few moments. All that really is needed is something in common—an interest, an ability, or a way of looking at the world. Or the point in common might be a conviction of calling, a sense of destiny. In the jungles of eastern Ecuador in the 1950s, missionaries could cut right to the core of what had brought them to this remote place. Some would wonder if they belonged there. Others would leave. And some would stay and persist in what they had come to do—find lost people and shine the light of Christ on them.

The vast miles of jungle in Ecuador were populated with multiple Indian tribes, each with its own culture and customs. People coming into the jungle from the outside could not make generalizations about what methods were effective for reaching Indian tribes, whether for commercial venture or missionary work. Each situation had its own special needs, its own unique dimensions.

The Quichuas were one of the largest of the jungle tribes, scattered over thousands of miles. The Aucas, by contrast, were one of the smallest tribes, perhaps numbering only a few hundred. While the Quichuas welcomed contact from the outside world, with the agricultural, educational, and medical benefits that came with such contact, the Aucas sent a consistent and clear message that they wanted the world to stay out of their territory. Rather than being curious about the white man, the Aucas were suspicious and quick to act on their suspicions. Even a company as powerful as the Shell Oil Company, which had prospected for oil in the jungle, had withdrawn in fear over this small tribe. Hostile Aucas had attacked a work crew and speared three workers to death. Understandably, the laborers had panicked, and it became difficult to find people willing to work in that setting. A year later, the company had lost eight more employees.

Profitability aside, prospecting for oil in that region simply was no longer feasible. The cost in human lives was too high. Shell elected to abandon the little towns its business had created. Buildings, airstrips, roads—they pulled their people out and left it all behind. Over the next few years, missionaries in several locations made creative and practical use of the assortment of materials left behind by Shell. For the missionaries, profitability was never a question. Instead, the violent behavior of the Aucas fueled the desire to penetrate their territory with Christianity.

In 1954 and 1955, a team of missionaries quietly assembled, pulled together by their common vision. Their task seemed beyond what was realistic—or beyond what was necessary. A small group of jungle Indians is a small target to reach, and their resistance made contact almost impossible. Was this the best use of missionary time and energy—to try to reach the Aucas? Other tribes were more populous and more receptive. Would it not have been better to invest resources in more fertile fields? No doubt these were some of the objectives raised by sensible people, both missionaries and their supporters.

Yet the team persisted, moving ahead one imperceptible step at a time.

Nate and Marj Saint had arrived in Ecuador in 1948, making them veteran missionaries by the time Pete, Jim, and Elisabeth arrived in 1952. They set up housekeeping in Shell Mera, a place where the Shell Oil Company had dug for oil and later abandoned when it was no longer profitable. Shell Oil had left behind some skeletal structures that formed an outline for what might become a mission station.

Almost as soon as he arrived, Nate began doing what he had come to Ecuador to do: fly a plane to ferry missionaries between stations and transport their cargo. Providing air service would save missionaries days or weeks of travel by foot or slow vehicle over rough roads. This was the objective of Missionary Aviation Fellowship, the organization under which Nate and Marj served. Nate was both pilot and maintenance man. He handled all the repairs himself. Marj became hostess to missionaries passing through Shell Mera en route to or from remote locations.

Nate was committed to safety, efficiency, and economy. Just because a plane was now available, missionaries could be no less selective about what they took with them on a journey. Nate watched weight limits carefully and made every ounce count. When the Piper Cub was purchased, it had seats that were padded and comfortable. But they also weighed eight pounds each. Nate chose to remove those seats and install harder, less comfortable seats that weighed only one pound each. The difference could be made up in extra cargo, every pound precious, on each trip the plane took, and it was well worth a few minutes of discomfort for his passengers.[1]

Nate was creative with improving the mechanical efficiency of the plane as well. He developed a back-up fuel system that would put the plane at less risk should the main fuel system fail for some reason. The whole rig, which provided immeasurable added safety, weighed less than four pounds.

Another of his innovations was a method of lowering a canvas bucket from the plane while it was in flight. Nate perfected the flight maneuvers necessary so that the bucket could be directed into the hands of someone waiting on the ground. He was able to deliver mail, medicines, and small packages without having to land the plane.

Whenever the plane was in the air or away from Shell Mera, Marj Saint maintained radio contact with Nate. She checked on weather conditions at whatever Nate's destination was and maintained daily contact with all the missionaries in the area. If there was an emergency and the plane was needed, Marj knew about it right away.

Over the years, the little house that Nate had built when he and Marj had arrived in Ecuador grew into a large chalet with spacious porches and running water.

They raised the roof and added a second story, which gave them a total of ten bedrooms and generous accommodations for missionaries passing through. Their home became a true refuge for missionaries living and working in more primitive conditions.

But they were not far from primitive areas themselves. Nate was aware that Auca Indians lived only sixty miles by air from Shell Mera. Occasionally, he used his plane for an aerial survey, curious about the exact location of the Aucas. But the tribe remained hidden from view.

Macuma was a mission station in the southern jungle. There, Roger and Barbara Youderian lived and worked among the Jívaro Indians. The Jívaros are famous around the world for their shrunken human heads. In the 1950s they inhabited a vast area of seven thousand square miles of jungle and had remained independent of the white men who ruled their country.

After serving in the army in World War II, Roger felt drawn to the mission field. He and Barbara became missionaries under the Gospel Missionary Union, a non-denominational mission board. They arrived in Ecuador in 1953 with a six-month-old daughter. After studying Spanish at Shell Mera with the Saints, the Youderians went to Macuma and joined another missionary couple in the work there. They plunged into language work and developed a method of teaching the Jívaros to read and write in their own language.

From there, they moved to Wambimi, where the Shell Oil Company had abandoned an airstrip and a few dilapidated houses. At Wambimi, Roger hoped to reach the

Atshuaras tribe, related linguistically to the Jívaros. Making friendly contact took some time, of course, because there were no missionaries already working among the Atshuaras. Roger eventually was successful and was able to preach to the Atshuaras, who understood the Jívaro language.

Roger Youderian did not shy away from a challenge. Repeatedly, he had proven his linguistic skills. He had put himself in dangerous situations for the sake of preaching the gospel. Yet it was difficult to say what had really come of his efforts. The results were so small when compared to the need. Unknown to any of his missionary colleagues, Roger was struggling with his effectiveness as a missionary and was even considering leaving the field. When Nate Saint asked if he might be interested in helping to find the Auca tribe and make contact with them, Roger thought perhaps this was the new challenge he needed. Roger agreed to be part of the project.

Ed and Marilou McCully had had a quick romance. They'd met shortly before Ed had begun ministering with Jim Elliot in Chester, Illinois, and sustained their relationship from a distance during the next few months. Within a short time they had been engaged, and then had married a few months after that. Only recently had Ed left law school and committed himself to missionary work, but this had been no deterrent for Marilou. Together, they'd taken the practical step of studying tropical diseases and their treatments, as well as obstetrics, dentistry, and medical fundamentals. Undistracted by the demands of marriage and family, Ed had fulfilled his pledge to Jim Elliot to go to Ecuador. The McCullys had arrived in Quito at the end of 1952 with an eight-month-old son.

Ed and Marilou were in Quito when the floods wiped out their future home in Shandia. As soon as Ed heard the radio transmission that the buildings had been destroyed, his instinct was to go immediately to Shandia to see if he could help. Marilou instantly agreed that he should go. Clearly Ed was needed in Shandia.

Slightly anxious about being separated from his wife and baby boy, Ed wanted to be sure Marilou was certain he should go. She assured him she and the baby would be fine and that she would sit right by the radio waiting for further information. Marilou accepted more than Ed's temporary absence; the unavoidable reality was that they would have to move to Shandia under much more primitive conditions than they had expected, but Ed and Marilou accepted this graciously. They displayed the adaptability and self-sacrifice that missionary life demands.

Jim Elliot had spoken to Ed often about the Aucas. Part of their dream of working together in the jungle included reaching the Aucas. Moving to Shandia put them one step closer. There, Ed and Marilou helped with the reconstruction and learned Quichua. The joint efforts of the McCullys, the Elliots, and Pete Fleming resulted in a fully functioning mission station with a school, a medical clinic, and a small store. Shandia was ready to serve as a hub for surrounding outstations. Jim and Elisabeth Elliot would run the station, as well as make preaching tours with other missionaries in outlying areas.

Jim and Elisabeth's commitment to Shandia freed

Ed and Marilou to move to Arajuno, the outstation that Ed had been developing. The Shell Oil Company had occupied Arajuno for a number of years and had established a small town for employees. When they'd abandoned Arajuno in 1949, Shell had left behind an excellent airstrip, making the missionary outstation immediately accessible. The Shell buildings had deteriorated beyond repair, but Ed was able to salvage some materials here and there. Opening an outstation would be fairly easy, compared to carving out a new spot in the jungle as Jim had done in Puyupungu.

At first, Ed flew to Arajuno on the weekends to preach to the hundred or so Quichuas who lived there. Eventually, he used some of his time to work on a home suitable for his family. He put the salvaged scraps to good use. He was ready to move Marilou and their two small sons to Arajuno—with some sensible precautions.

Arajuno was on the edge of the territory occupied by the Aucas and had been the site of several brutal incidents during the Shell Oil years. Even the Quichuas feared the Aucas and were not exempt from their attacks. The Quichuas persistently reminded the McCullys of the danger they were in by choosing to live in the abandoned town. With the help of Nate Saint, Ed installed an electric security fence thirty yards from the house in every direction. This gave the family a refuge beyond the range that an Auca spear could be thrown.

Under Jim Elliot's influence to go into mission work as an unattached man, Pete Fleming had left his engagement behind and come to Ecuador in 1952. After Jim got engaged to Elisabeth, Pete decided to finally become

147

engaged to Olive. And after Jim and Elisabeth married, Pete went back to the States to marry Olive. When he returned to Ecuador with Olive, they spent a year in Quito for Olive's turn to learn Spanish. After all this time, Pete Fleming was ready to return to the jungle with his bride. He had been away from Shandia for fifteen months. The Indians there welcomed Pete back heartily, hoping he would stay. But the Elliots had things well in hand in Shandia; Pete and Olive would soon move on.

Pete's first task, however, was to help Jim with an intensive three-week Bible institute for the Quichuas. They covered Bible history and content, basic doctrine, and personal evangelism. Pete's gifts for teaching flared and brought him great satisfaction.

Within a few weeks, Pete and Olive moved into their long-term task. Their assignment now was the outstation at Puyupungu, where they lived in the house that Jim and Elisabeth had built but occupied only for a few weeks. Grateful for the shelter, their existence was nevertheless primitive, even for Pete, who had lived in the jungle before. The plane had to make several trips to get their gear in, and even then housekeeping was at minimal level.

Olive still faced the task of learning yet another language, but Pete was able to begin teaching from the Bible in Quichua. They battled the habitual drunken behavior during fiestas, but gradually Pete's natural gift for teaching bore fruit. He progressed to the point of speaking about baptism and establishing a meeting time for new believers.

Olive, with her medical training, now took over the

medical side of the work. Because she did not know Quichua, however, she would often have to write down the sounds she heard the patients utter, then take the notes to Pete and hope that what she had written down were actual words that he could translate. Despite this cumbersome procedure, the gift of medical care seemed to break down barriers of fear between the Flemings and the Indians.[2]

Five missionary couples now were poised to reach the Aucas, all of them living on the outskirts of the area the Aucas occupied. Jim and Elisabeth had even discussed the possibility that they would go and live among the Aucas once friendly contact had been established. Many details of the Aucas were unknown—including their exact location. Their habit was to remain hidden deep in the jungle and silently surprise those whom they attacked. Very few Aucas experienced individual friendly contact with outsiders.

Nate Saint looked for chances to search for the Aucas from the air as he flew his regular routes over the jungle. But the forest was too thick; it was almost impossible to see anything. Almost.

They did not give up.

SIXTEEN

They were on their knees, but they were not praying. They raised their hands and gestured, but it was not in praise.

Instead, Nate Saint, Ed McCully, and Jim Elliot, along with another missionary pilot named Johnny Keenan, were poring over a map of the jungles of eastern Ecuador. It was September of 1955, and they had decided that it was time to begin looking for the Aucas in earnest. They knew they were all living on the edges of Auca territory, yet for months they had not been able to put a finger on the map and point to the place where the Aucas lived. But they were getting close, and missionary zeal surged a dream toward reality.

Although they did not know the location of the Aucas, the missionaries were painfully aware of what they did know—the temperament of the Aucas. That this particular Indian tribe was known for its brutality made reaching them a sensitive matter. Not only would the men be putting themselves at risk, but if other mission groups knew about what they were doing, interference and publicity could devastate their plans. Some would object to their plan as too dangerous. Others would want to join—and perhaps control—a sensitive operation. The project had to be kept small, confined only to those whose commitment was unquestioned. Jim Elliot had committed to finding the Aucas several years earlier, and had carried in his vision the help of Pete Fleming and Ed McCully, whom he seemed to have personally recruited with this goal in mind. Once in Ecuador, he had met Nate Saint and discovered a mirror image of his own passion. Nate brought Roger Youderian to the team, and the inner circle was complete. Other than their wives, no one else would know what they were doing—not their families in the States, nor the mission organizations they served.

In the meantime, within the secrecy of their own small circle, the missionaries began gathering as much background information on the Aucas as they could find. No one knows for sure when the savagery of the Aucas began. But as far back as 1541, a Spanish explorer encountered hostile Indians who killed some of his men. In the next century, Jesuit missionaries met the same fate. After that, few people ventured from the outside into the territory occupied by these obscure Indian tribes.

The Industrial Revolution changed all that. Modern parts of the world needed rubber, and the Amazonian basin in South America was one of the best places to get rubber. Unfortunately, the rubber-hunters were interested purely in the profit they could make if they supplied rubber. They had no use for an exchange of culture or peaceful cohabitation. Instead, they deceived the Indians by friendly gestures, then raided their villages and enslaved young men to work on the rubber-producing haciendas. Whole villages were slaughtered so that the Indians would not interfere with the production of rubber. Despite the later efforts of a Jesuit missionary, the animosity between the Indians and the white men from the outside was too far advanced. This territory could not be colonialized as other parts of the country had.[1]

A valuable source of information for Jim and the others was a man known as Don Carlos Sevilla. He ran a hacienda only a few minutes from Shandia by air, but before that he had lived and worked in the Auca territory for twenty-six years. He had firsthand information about what the Aucas would do. He had lost workers repeatedly, and he himself had barely survived an attack that had left him physically scarred. Once, while he had been away getting medicines for Indian families working for him, the Aucas had descended and killed everyone but a young boy who had been left for dead.

A few years later, Don Carlos and his Indian workers had been attacked two times within four months. On the river in their canoes, they had been targets for dozens of Auca lances, and there was little they could do to defend themselves. The canoe had overturned and five peaceful Quichuas had been killed. A decade later, another attack finally pushed Don Carlos out of Auca territory. By the time he met Jim Elliot and the other missionaries, another twenty years had passed. Still, Don Carlos did not consider that it was impossible to reenter the Auca territory. He had both advice and encouragement to offer the younger men. He thought that, with the right strategy, the Aucas might accept friendship. It would take a long time, but it could be done.[2] His cautious but optimistic outlook spurred the missionaries on.

As they talked to other people, though, the missionaries soon found that many disagreed with Don Carlos. In their view, the Aucas would never tolerate white men on their land, and it was foolish to try. Perhaps this was so for people motivated by making money off of the natural resources in the Auca area. But might it be different for someone who came with different motives? Could missionaries, who only wanted to give and did not want to take, convince the Aucas that they were no threat?

Why the Aucas were so savage was a mystery that the missionaries could not unravel. The record of their attacks offered no pattern. Sometimes they killed and then robbed, but other times, they left behind valuable items and gave no clear reason for their killing. Everyone who was not an Auca was a white man, and no white man was safe.

Even the Aucas themselves were not safe. Sometimes a feud would break out within the tribe, and anger quickly gave way to killing fellow tribesmen. Whole extended families could be wiped out in a short period of time because one of its members angered someone in another family. Killing was not accidental; Auca boys were trained to do this. Don Carlos told the missionaries of having come upon a deserted Auca village and finding a life-size human figure made of balsa wood, with heart and face clearly outlined. The entire model had been riddled with lance marks. Clearly it had been used for practice in throwing lances and hitting a precise target.[3] The habit and skill of killing were systematically passed to each generation.

Thoroughly aware of these realities, the young missionaries continued planning their friendly "attack," and their search for the mysterious Aucas. Nate had been looking for them from the air for many months, even years, never knowing if he was getting any closer.

In the middle of September 1955, Nate made a routine flight to deliver vegetables to the McCullys in Arajuno. The day was bright and clear, a perfect morning for an aerial search of the jungle. Nate decided to do more than deliver vegetables that day. But two sets of eyes were better than one, so he recruited Ed's help. As soon as the cargo was unloaded, Nate and Ed raided Marilou's supplies for canned food and other emergency equipment. Within thirty minutes of landing, Nate was in the sky again, this time with Ed in the seat beside him.

They flew east from Arajuno, following the Nusho River. About fifty miles out, they turned north toward the Napo River. Between them they could scan a path eight miles wide. They saw what they always saw: miles and miles of dense, green, impenetrable forest. A passenger interested in sight-seeing would be impressed with the breath-taking lush beauty. Seeing the jungle from the air was an experience wholly different than trekking through it on the ground. Ed and Nate were not oblivious to this perspective, but they were not in search of inspiration. They were in search of Aucas. What they needed to see was a break in the trees, a patch of brown relieving the unrelenting green, or a wisp of smoke pointing to a village cooking fire.

Nate had done this countless times; it was not the

first time for Ed, either. Each time they flew, they knew this might be the time they would see the Aucas. Or it might not be; probably it would not be. It seemed that this bright September morning would be like all the other scouting trips. Nate eyed the fuel gauge; he did not have enough gas to go much farther. But the day was so perfect. It was frustrating to think of giving up when they had come so far out and visibility was so good. Nate calculated they could go a few more minutes.

Then they spotted something. Actually, Nate spotted it first; Ed was not sure there was anything to be seen. But Nate thought it was worth a closer look. He headed for what looked like nothing more than a slight blur on the landscape. But it was more. Once they got closer, they could see it was a clearing, no doubt about it. Nate looked at the gas gauge again. They could fly another fifteen minutes before going into reserve fuel, at which point they absolutely had to head back to Arajuno. So for fifteen minutes they circled the area, discovering more than a dozen similar clearings and a few houses. At last their patience had paid off. But they would have to be patient still longer. The excitement of that day had to be restrained by reality. They would be out of fuel soon and were unprepared to make closer contact with a people they knew very little about. Nate and Ed would have to talk to the others, keep thinking, and proceed carefully.[4] But it was now clear that Arajuno should be the base for further outreach to the Aucas. The McCully house would now be a strategy center as well as a home.

A couple of weeks later, Nate had to fly Pete Fleming and Jim Elliot to an area where they planned to preach to a group of Quichuas they had not reached before. In order to transport Pete, Jim, their guides, and their gear, Nate would have to fly over the Auca area a total of four times. This was a perfect opportunity for further scouting, and Nate intended to make maximum use of it.

Jim, of course, was eager to see what Nate and Ed had seen. He had waited too many years for the sight of an Auca to flinch about a few extra minutes in the air. He was the first to be transported to the preaching station, and he fixed his eyes on the jungle below. Aching to see some sign of life, he scanned the blanket of thick green, looking for any small relief in the thick jungle covering. But he saw nothing on that trip. Jim simply had to rely on what Nate and Ed had seen, and continue his patient waiting.

On the next trip, with Pete as his passenger, Nate saw some clearings not far outside Arajuno. Only fifteen minutes by air from where Ed McCully lived were half a dozen large Auca houses and a scattering of smaller ones. This was a different set of clearings than Ed and Nate had discovered previously. Now they had found the second main group of the tribe. The missionaries had searched for months and seen nothing. After the long wait, in the space of half a month, they had discovered major portions of the tribe. Now they could put their fingers on the map and point to where they wanted to be.

Years before all this happened, a young Auca girl had escaped a tribal feud and emerged from the Auca territory. Dayuma had been a teenager when both of her parents and her brothers and sisters had been killed. She had survived the attack by hiding, and then had known that her best chance for safety was to flee to the Quichuas. As an unarmed young female, she had been accepted as no threat and given shelter. Eventually, Dayuma had found her way to Don Carlos's hacienda, where he had given her a job. It was there that Jim Elliot encountered her.

Dayuma was a wealth of information for the eager missionaries. She could describe in detail Auca ways of living and hunting. The Aucas were incredible trackers, surveying every intrusion into their territory with such skill that the outsiders never knew they were being observed. They developed expertise in reading footprints and knowing just who had passed by. For instance, Dayuma told Don Carlos that every step he had taken years ago in Auca territory had been observed; they had always known where he was. The Aucas knew everything about the Shell camp at Arajuno where the McCullys now lived.[5] No doubt the McCullys themselves were under constant silent surveillance.

Perhaps the greatest help Dayuma gave was to teach Jim some vocabulary of the Auca language. Jim, of course, did not tell Dayuma why he was so curious about her people. And Dayuma probably realized she was an oddity and was used to answering questions from people about the strange ways of the Aucas.

The hacienda where Dayuma worked was only a four-hour trek from Shandia, where Jim lived. To Jim, and in the context of the jungle, this was a short distance that was no obstacle. He took his notebook and list of phrases he wanted to learn and went to see Dayuma.

Dayuma cooperated beautifully, patiently helping

him with his pronunciation. He copiously wrote down the sounds in his notebook so he could reproduce them later. Before he left Dayuma, Jim could say, "I like you. I want to be your friend," "I want to approach you," "What is your name?" and a handful of other phrases he would be able to use to extend friendship to the Aucas.

But even Dayuma could not solve the mystery of why the Aucas killed with such predictability and such little provocation. "Never trust them," she said emphatically. "They may appear friendly and then they will turn around and kill."[6]

The team now had the location of the Aucas, key phrases to communication, a base of operations in Arajuno, and heightened motivation to proceed with their plans to reach an unreachable tribe. The vision that Jim Elliot had carried since college was coming to light.

SEVENTEEN

Now the adrenaline flowed. Individual members of the team reinforced the vision for each other and gave substance to what had previously only been a subject of conversation, not action. "Operation Auca" was in full swing. Nate, with his plane, and Ed, who lived nearest the Auca settlements, made weekly flights over the Auca area. Nate rigged a mechanism to the plane that would let them lower a bucket and drop its contents within reach of the Aucas without ever having to land the plane. As often as he could, Jim went along on these flights. Their strategy was to become a familiar sight above the Aucas and be perceived as bearers of gifts and useful items.

The first gift was dropped on October 6, 1955, and it was a small aluminum kettle with a lid. Inside it, the missionaries put an assortment of bright buttons that the Aucas, who wore no clothing, could use as ornaments. Then they tied on ribbons to make the bucket look festive and friendly, and they were ready to go. Although they did not see any Aucas on that flight, they did see houses, a clearing, and evidence that the area was occupied. The Aucas themselves remained hidden in the forest.

Probably Nate's Piper was not the first airplane the Aucas had seen. The Shell Oil Company had used planes, taking off and landing at the airstrip in Arajuno. During the years that Shell had operated in the area, the Aucas had learned what the company was doing and why it was there. But how would the Aucas react to a new plane, full of strangers whose motives were not known? The missionaries left their gifts on a sand bar, with no one in sight, and flew back to Arajuno, not knowing whether the pot and buttons had been found, or whether they had been appreciated or thrown into the river in disgust.

On the next week's flight, Nate's plan was to check the sand bar and see if the first gift was gone. They were pleased to see that the gift was gone. It was possible that it had been carried away by the river rather than picked up by the Indians. However, the area looked well occupied, so most likely the pot had been picked up.

The second gift was a machete. They had heard that the Aucas would kill for a machete, literally, so obviously this would be a valuable gift. They chose a new spot to let down the machete, not wanting to create jealousy among the Aucas by always leaving gifts at the same clearing.

Ed was with Nate again on this flight, leaning out of the plane with binoculars to look for signs of life. Again the Aucas remained hidden—except for one. Ed saw his first Auca that day. He was moving around the clearing, but not trying to hide like his tribesmen. In a few minutes two others appeared and peered up into the sky at the plane. Now Ed and Nate felt sure that their first gift had been received and that these men thought the plane might leave something else. They let down the machete with glee, then flew home to Arajuno.

Back at Arajuno, Ed discovered that the Aucas had come quite close to his house. Local Indians told him they had seen Auca tracks around the camp. All along, everyone had thought that most likely the McCullys were under observation. Now they knew for sure. This could be dangerous for the family and the entire team if they made a wrong move. They did not know what trivial activity might provoke the Aucas to swift action. On the other hand, it gave the men the opportunity to link Ed with the weekly flights. They made a wooden model of the airplane and hung it outside the McCully house. Now anyone watching the house would know Ed was one of the gift-givers.

When they made the third weekly flight, Nate had difficulty regaining altitude after the gift drop. He soon saw that the Aucas had taken hold of the line on which the bucket hung and seemed reluctant to let go. Finally someone broke the line and the plane was free.[1]

Curiosity in the settlement swelled. The next week, there were more Aucas waiting for the flight. Jim was able to go on this fourth flight, and he had his phrase cards handy. Using a battery-powered loudspeaker, Jim shouted out in the Auca language, "I like you! I am your friend! I like you! You will be given a pot." Then he dropped another gift and waited for the Auca reaction.

Jim wrote later: "First time I ever saw an Auca—

fifteen hundred feet is a long ways if you're looking out of an airplane. . . . We saw perhaps eight Indians scurrying around the house. One crossed the river with something on his head and seemed to flash a new machete. I did not see him return even though it looked as though he only went to the *chagra* (plantation). One rushed into the house and returned with a lance. But when we dropped the machete on the string, they tore off both machete and the small basket we had tied on to receive some exchange. . . . At this a group raced back into the trees behind the house and one lone man walked to the beach. He cupped his hand. We dropped a small aluminum pot, with ribbons. It contained a yellow shirt and beads. The man on the beach pointed to the place of the fall. Those behind the house got it, and one was soon flailing the yellow shirt." [2]

Encouraged by the friendly response their "visits" were stirring up, Nate, Jim, and Ed conferred and decided the time was right for the next phase of Operation Auca—ground contact. The response of the Aucas continued to encourage them.

On the next trip, Ed McCully used the microphone to call out, "We like you! We like you! We have come to pay a visit!" The Aucas answered by dancing and reaching their hands out toward Ed's extended hands, as he leaned out the door of the plane.[3] They made plans to consolidate the team and move ahead. They would continue the weekly air trips dropping gifts for several more weeks. Then they would make ground contact.

Whenever Ed was unable to make the regular flights with Nate, Jim was eager to fill in. The sightings excited him and propelled him toward the Aucas.

After about two months of weekly flights, Jim wrote: "Nate and I made my second Auca flight. . . . Noticed an increased amount of cutting down the forest and land clearing since my last visit. They seem to know what to do with machetes and axes. . . . The second house has a model airplane carved on the house ridge, and there we dropped a machete, a pair of short pants, and I saw a thing that thrilled me. It seemed an old man stood beside the house and waved with both his arms as if to signal us to come down. Aucas waving at me to come! At the next house, they have made a large clearing and built a bamboo platform on which one—a white-shirted one—stood and waved. . . . Nate was in a hurry as it was late afternoon, and he stepped it up. God send me soon to the Aucas."[4]

The single-mindedness that had characterized Jim Elliot's college years had not ebbed over the years. Quichua work, marriage, even fatherhood had not blurred his vision. Over the years, his journals echoed the desire for God to take him to the Aucas. He was getting close.

But life outside Operation Auca continued. During these weeks of regular flights, Pete was occupied at Puyu-pungu, and Jim's work at Shandia continued and thrived. Quichua leaders and preachers emerged and flourished under Jim's instruction. He worked steadily on the school and reinforced the house he and Elisabeth lived in with their baby daughter. Their garden was finally starting to produce.

Jim and Pete continued their outings to preach to other groups of Quichuas. Jim had plenty of work; the task at Shandia was far from complete. But the routine work was punctuated with the extra excitement of contact with the Aucas. Jim's impulses were divided at a practical level. While conscientiously pouring himself into everything at Shandia, the Aucas were never far from his mind.

He carried note cards filled with Auca phrases in his pocket so he could use odd moments to practice them. Sometimes they were the last things he looked at before he went to bed. All the while he wondered why the opportunity to reach the Aucas had come when it did. Did God really mean for Jim and Elisabeth to leave Shandia already?

Elisabeth had the same question. She was keenly aware of the dangers of Operation Auca, and though she was willing to risk whatever God asked her to risk, she did not want to make a foolish mistake. Was God really calling Jim to go to the Aucas at this point in time? She pressed him. "Are you sure you are supposed to go?" Jim's simple response was that he was called. After that Elisabeth was sure also. She got aggressively involved in the linguistic work with Dayuma to increase Jim's ability to communicate. They discussed going to live among the Aucas as a family if friendly ground contact was possible.[5]

Jim, Ed, and Nate agreed that they should soon take the next step, although they had varying views on what the next step should be. Nate favored continuing methodically with slowly increasing contact. Nothing was to be gained by rushing in prematurely, and much could be lost. Ed thought they should concentrate on finding and clearing an airstrip so they could eventually land the plane within a few miles of the Auca village.

Jim was the most impatient one of the three. He thought the time was right and pressed the team to move ahead with specific plans for ground contact. Pete Fleming, who was not part of the weekly flights but conferred regularly with the other three, was not convinced the time was right. The hatred that the Aucas had held toward the white men had been going on for centuries. As much as he wanted to reach the Aucas with the gospel, Pete was not sure it was wise to assume that this obstacle had been overcome in just a few weeks of dropping gifts from an airplane. Though Jim had learned a few phrases and was teaching them to the others, their use of Auca language was far from adequate to communicate without confusion. Pete argued it would be better to spend more time learning language from Dayuma before risking face-to-face contact.[6]

It was at this time that Roger Youderian entered the picture at Nate's invitation. The others had not met Roger, but they knew about his work and trusted Nate's recommendation.

As Operation Auca hurtled toward Christmas, it was clear that Ed, Jim, and Roger intended to attempt ground contact very soon. They would go by canoe, with two Quichua guides and gear to set up camp, so space was limited. This meant they could take one other man—either Nate or Pete. The team of four would set up temporary housekeeping on a beach along the river, as close as possible to where they knew the Aucas were. Nate had been strategic in locating the Aucas, but Pete had also been committed to reaching the Aucas. They would have to decide which one of them would go.

In the meantime, Nate kept up with the regular

flights and gift-dropping, while everyone prayed for the miraculous breakthrough they believed was only a few weeks away.

EIGHTEEN

Before long, the Aucas had deciphered the seven-day cycle of Nate's flights and now stood in the clearings or on the rooftops awaiting the aerial visits. The individuals who had greeted the early flights now were accompanied by more and more of their fellow tribesmen. A few proudly wore the occasional item of clothing that the missionaries dropped—T-shirts, shorts, or pants.

Nate could lower the plane to within two hundred feet of an Auca and detect no sign of alarm, only welcome curiosity and friendly facial expressions. The one-sided gift-giving became mutual. With secure square knots, the Aucas tied return gifts onto the line Nate and Ed used to drop their tokens of friendship. The missionary machetes were exchanged for feathered headdresses and cotton string and small animals that the missionaries presumably were supposed to eat. One time the Aucas tied on a colorful parrot in a basket. The bird survived the treacherous journey and became a pet for the missionary children.

The men were getting anxious to make ground contact. The time seemed right. Not once had the Aucas reacted to the flights negatively or with any behavior that should alarm the Americans. The increasing curiosity of the Indians propelled the missionaries into action. Surely the Aucas were waiting for something more, something that would give meaning to the strange events in the air. At the same time, though, the missionaries knew it would be foolish to rush in without carefully thinking through a plan—and a back-up plan. It was critical that they try to anticipate any turn of events and decide ahead of time what they would do in these circumstances. They could not control what the Aucas might do, but they could control their own responses.

From their respective stations, Jim and Ed corresponded to share their developing thoughts. Believing that it was reasonably safe—they could never be 100 percent sure—Ed began thinking through what they would have to do. For instance, if the missionaries went in and set up a temporary camp along the river, they should not wait indefinitely for the Aucas to come to them. If the Aucas did not come to them willingly within a few days, the team should leave. They also should be prepared to abandon the effort if they encountered any reluctance or resistance on the part of the Aucas. They would be sure to identify themselves clearly with the plane the Aucas had come to expect; they could not assume that the Aucas would automatically connect the white strangers on the ground with the gifts dropped from the plane. Given the Auca's history of hostility

toward white people, clear identification was essential.
For instance, they could wear the headdresses that the
Aucas had given them, and carry model airplanes. And
they could carry more gifts and be ready to use the
phrases they had been memorizing: *Biti miti punimupa!*
I like you![1]

And what would they do to protect themselves if the
situation got dangerous? Realistically, they had to admit
that they still knew very little about the Aucas and what
motivated their behavior. Centuries of savagery were not
erased by a few weeks of curiosity and token gifts. Though
the missionaries had every reason to believe the Aucas
would welcome them and that they could proceed—cautiously—with further overtures of friendship, nothing was
certain. The Aucas could turn on the team without warn-
ing, and they were experts with spears. What would the
missionaries do then?

They discussed the question thoroughly and decided
they would take guns. One strong reason for taking
guns was the possibility of being attacked by wild animals. But only the missionaries would have the guns, not
the Quichuas who might go to help set up the camp. And
the guns would be out of sight, where they would not
alarm the Aucas. The Aucas were isolated from civilization, but surely they had seen guns during the colonial
years or while Shell Oil had been in the area. If the Aucas
saw that the missionaries had guns, they might jump to
the wrong conclusion about how the missionaries
planned to use the weapons. The team did not want to
fire a gun while the Aucas were near. If they were forced
to fire because of Auca hostility, everything they had
worked for would collapse. Only in an extreme situation

would they fire a gun, and then only to frighten the Aucas, not to harm them.[2] They were unanimous in the conviction that they should not use guns to save their own lives. But no one seriously thought that situation would come up.

The original plan was to go into Auca territory in canoes on the Curaray River with Quichua guides. As the planning progressed, Nate began to think that it might be possible to go in by air. This would take less time and would mean the project would not have to involve the Quichuas. If they could land the plane, they could set up a little makeshift house on a beach. Nate could go in and out every day with supplies and information while the others waited patiently for the Aucas to come to them. In the meantime, the team would not be so cut off from help, if they needed it.

Now that he knew where the Aucas were, Nate began scouting the area with a new objective: to find a beach along the river that would not have to be cleared before the plane could land. He found several possibilities and quickly narrowed the choice. This place, which they would call "Palm Beach," was less than five miles from where the Aucas were settled. It should not take long for the Aucas to discover the missionaries were there.

Jim Elliot's construction experience now became very important. It was his task to put together the pieces of a "prefabricated" house that the team could construct in a tree. The height would give them added security at night, especially with a gasoline lamp burning at the foot of the tree. Jim was also in charge of arms and ammunition, while Nate set up the communication and transportation systems. Roger made up the first-aid kit, and Ed collected items that they could trade with the Aucas.

Nate would fly in the pieces for the tree house and other supplies and let them free fall to a soft landing on the beach. Then he would fly in Ed, Jim, and Roger, who would put the house together, clear a couple of trees from the beach to improve the landing strip, and begin the wait.

It was during the Christmas holidays that an urgent message crackled over the radio. Marilou McCully, alone at Arajuno with two small children and pregnant with a third, sent word to Marj Saint that a Quichua guard had spotted a naked Auca with a lance standing barely fifty yards from the McCully house.

To the horror of the Quichua guard, Marilou refused to give him ammunition for a gun. Instead, Marilou had tried to follow the Auca, calling out friendly phrases and carrying a gift.

Ed and Nate flew from Shell Mera to Arajuno immediately, of course, but by the time they got there all that remained of the visitor was his footprint. But he had been there. Ground contact with the Aucas might come sooner than any of them realized—and perhaps not according to their plan.

They set the date for January 3, 1956. If they did not go then, they would have to wait until after the rainy season, and no one wanted to wait several more months. Some of the details still had to be finalized, though. For instance, going in by air meant that they did not have to limit the team to four members. Jim, Roger Youderian, Ed, and Nate were all committed to going. Pete was still undecided.

Pete had participated in the planning but had not committed himself to the actual operation. More than four years had passed since Pete Fleming had pledged himself to primitive mission work with Jim Elliot. From the beginning, he had shared the dream of reaching the Aucas with Jim. During that time, however, he had realized that he was not physically rugged enough for extended work in the jungle, and he had married Olive. More was at risk than his own safety. Olive, however, did not want to stand in his way. If Pete truly believed God wanted him to be part of Operation Auca, he should go.

At the last planning meeting in Arajuno during the Christmas holidays of 1955, Pete was pressed to make his decision. But he still was not sure whether he had a role. He did not want to go if he could not make a legitimate contribution.

Though Jim Elliot had come to the jungle with Pete as single partners sharing the same goal, now he was not sure Pete should go to Palm Beach. His argument was that if something did happen to the team and Jim, Ed, and Pete were all lost, there would be no man left who could speak Quichua, and that would put at risk all the work they had done so far among the Quichuas.

At this point, Ed McCully interjected, objecting to Jim's conjecture that something might happen. Ed had two small sons, and his wife was seven months pregnant with their third child. He reminded everyone that his family had been living on Auca land for almost a year with no incidents. The team was taking every reasonable precaution. Ed said that if he thought he might be killed, he would not go. So Jim's argument that they should safeguard at least one Quichua-speaking male missionary did not hold weight in Ed's mind.

Pete still did not know what his role would be, and he would not go if he could not really help. Nate Saint, however, had pegged Pete for a job weeks ago in his own mind. He was simply waiting for Pete to declare his intentions. Nate wanted some help on the flights in and out of Palm Beach. Because Pete was the lightest of the men, taking him would make the maneuvers easier than carrying a heavier person. Assurance that he would be useful was all Pete needed at that point. He decided to go. The team was complete.[3]

The men had decided what they were going to do. The women still had to come to terms with what it might mean for them. Despite Ed's conviction that the risk was minimal, the women knew that becoming widows was a serious possibility.

Elisabeth Elliot and Olive Fleming talked one evening. Olive admitted her uneasy feelings; who could really know what might happen? Elisabeth and Jim had talked about living among the Aucas as a family, and Elisabeth was still prepared to do that, even if later it turned out to be risky. In her mind, it would be better to die with Jim, if that was what was going to happen.[4]

On January 2 Nate radioed to Jim at Shandia that since the weather was good, he wanted to shuttle Jim to Arajuno that day, a day earlier than planned. Elisabeth helped him pack his things, including items that might help entertain the Aucas and give the men time to establish the friendly contact they needed. Obviously, the men would not be able to converse with the Aucas at any length. Though they had all memorized the phrases that Jim and Elisabeth had gathered, they would soon run out of things to say. They needed nonverbal ways of making friends. Jim packed a harmonica, a View-Master with pictures, and a yo-yo, as well as some practical items, such as a snakebite kit, a flashlight, and the Auca language material.[5]

Elisabeth held her tongue as Jim headed out the door of their house. She wanted to say, "Do you realize you may never open that door again?" But she didn't. She walked him out to the plane, where he kissed her good-bye as if he were taking a simple vegetable run, hopped in next to the pilot, and flew off.[6] Elisabeth watched the plane disappear from view as the sound of its engine grew faint.

That night, the five men gathered in Arajuno: Ed McCully, Nate Saint, Roger Youderian, Pete Fleming, and Jim Elliot. The time for theoretical strategies was past. Now they really had to sort through the details that would make their plan work. Every movement they would make the next day had to be planned out in detail. They made copious lists of equipment for each of the flights into Palm Beach the next day. Certain items should go in first to begin a shelter and set up house-keeping. Then less essential items would follow.

They checked and double-checked their equipment. They tinkered with the schedule for the day, trying to decide just when to make the multiple flights required to get everything and everyone into Palm Beach. Nate had to make maximum use of the daylight hours and still leave time to get himself and Pete back to Arajuno before dark.

After hours of planning, the details were in place.
They were as ready as they were ever going to be.

No one slept much that night.

NINETEEN

Operation Auca got off to a good start on January 3, 1956, right on schedule. The plan called for Ed and Nate to make the first flight at eight in the morning, and they were airborne right on time. Nate had calmly managed an early morning crisis regarding brake fluid. Now they faced fog—fog that got thicker as they progressed along the river. Nate remained hopeful they would be able to land the plane. Just as they approached their target, the fog thinned enough that they were able to drop to a lower altitude and attempt a landing. Conscious of the risk they were taking in landing on an unfamiliar beach, they flew over the beach once, checking for any obstructions that could endanger the plane when it landed.

Nate had planned to make several passes over the beach before landing, but the beach was clear and there was no reason to wait. They landed on the second pass. Grateful for a safe, precise landing between two trees,

Nate brought the plane to a halt.

Although they had surveyed the strip of beach as thoroughly as they could, from the air they could never be sure what the sand would be like. Now they found that it was softer than they had hoped for. As they came to a stop, they were only a few feet from the water, and they could feel the weight of the plane sinking into the sand. For a moment, their stomachs were in their throats. But the sand held. It was just firm enough to keep the plane from flipping over.

Ecstatic finally to be on Palm Beach, Nate and Ed jumped out of the plane, unloaded the gear, and ran up and down the stretch of beach looking for smaller hazards that might cause a problem in the future. So far, everything was going according to plan.

The next hurdle would be to see if Nate could take off again. The sand was too soft to take off; the plane's wheels would not move. Nate could not taxi to gain speed before lifting off. Ed and Nate had to push the plane back into some bushes, where the ground was firmer, and Nate had to take off from there. He had less space to taxi now, so he would have to get airborne quickly. The lift was successful, and while Nate headed back to Arajuno for the second scheduled load, Ed McCully was left alone on an Auca beach, standing in awe of the challenge the team faced, and exposed and unarmed against threats from Auca or animal.

The less-than-perfect first landing and take-off meant that the team had to reconsider some of the careful plans from the night before. Under these precarious conditions, some of the equipment they had laid out was no longer essential. They started all over again with prioritizing what should go next.

On the second flight, Nate took Jim and Roger to Palm Beach. Now there were three men on the beach with minimal equipment and no way to contact Arajuno or Shell Mera. But the beach was only a few minutes by air from Arajuno, and Nate had calculated to the minute how long each flight would take.

On the third trip, he took in the radio, some tools, and the basics they needed to start work on the tree house. No doubt the radio—eventually they would have two—made everyone feel more secure. If something went wrong or someone was injured, they could get help within a few minutes.

After that, Nate continued with personal items, food, boards, and aluminum.[1] The day's work was done for Nate. The men on the beach moved into an aggressive work mode and began construction, all the while keeping their eyes and ears open to any sign that the Aucas were near. They slept thirty-five feet off the ground that night, safe from whatever might prowl around the base of the tree.

Jubilant to be on the beach, Jim's thoughts were still with Elisabeth, and he wrote her a note that Nate could take back on his next flight. He kept her informed of the obstacles they had encountered with take-offs and wrote of the beauties of the jungle—and the battle with mosquitoes at night. His tone was one of hope that perhaps that day would be the day they would reach the Aucas and his vision would be brought to maturity.

The waiting began. The men were settled on the beach, Nate and Pete were flying in and out every day, and radio contact with Marj Saint at Shell Mera was clear.

They were ready. But where were the Aucas? The men felt sure they were being watched, and the gifts that they left on the beach were picked up during the dark nights, but they never actually saw any Aucas on the beach.

Nate and Pete could see from the air whether the Aucas were making any movement toward Palm Beach. On Thursday, January 5, they saw only a few women and children walking around the Auca settlement. Where were the men who usually stood on the rooftops and greeted the plane? Then, as they landed, Nate and Pete saw clear human footprints near the beach—and not just one or two. There was no question but that the Aucas were nearby.

The sighting of footprints livened things up. Not sure whether to believe that the footprints were human, Roger and Jim now ran downstream along the beach to inspect them at close range. They found footprints of various sizes. They were several days old, but they showed clearly that the Aucas had been near Palm Beach. This was reason to think they would come again, and this spurred the team on, fueling excitement while straining patience.

The men had to keep waiting. With their camp established, they had little to do to pass the time. Jim read aloud from a novel, and they lolled in the shallow water for relief from the heat and insects.

When Nate and Pete left for the day, they tried to fly over the Auca settlement to give the Aucas some clue as to where to find the missionary camp. They were encouraged to see a man on a platform kneeling toward the direction of the camp site and pointing. If the Aucas knew where they were, surely they would come, or so the missionaries thought.

The next day, their third on the beach, brought more of the same routine. Pete and Nate flew in to spend the day on Palm Beach. The men prepared their meals in a makeshift cooking shelter and took turns stationing themselves along the beach and shouting Auca phrases into the jungle. If the Aucas were indeed as near as the missionaries thought, the breakthrough could come at any minute.

Adrenaline flowed as they fought against the possibility that the Aucas could be near and yet choose not to come out onto the beach. They put to use every friendly, encouraging construction they had learned in the Auca language.

Abruptly a male voice answered one of their calls. Although they had been hoping for such a response, they were still surprised when it came. Three Aucas stepped out of the trees and into clear view, a young man and two women, one only a teenager.

Immediately on their feet and attentive, the missionaries managed to continue with the Auca phrases: *Puinani!* Welcome! The Aucas stood on the opposite side of the river, examining the strange outsiders.

The man began to talk, but obviously the missionaries could not keep up with his flow. They had already used up the extent of their Auca language and had never really had any practice in listening to Aucas speak. So they had to depend on non-verbal communication. The man's gestures were more important than his words.

Finally, the light went on for the missionaries. The man was offering the teenage girl to them, perhaps in trade or perhaps as a gift. And the Aucas wanted

Jim ELLIOT

someone to come across the river.

Once he understood this, Jim Elliot wasted no time in stripping to his shorts and plunging into the water. The others cautioned him—and rightfully so. This was an unknown and unpredictable situation. By separating himself from the group, Jim was putting himself beyond the help of his colleagues. Once he got to the other side, Jim would be separated from the other four and on his own. If he should be attacked, no one could help him.

Jim slowed down a bit, trying to decide the best thing to do. He did not think he would be attacked. He continued his forward progress slowly. In response, the girl stepped off a log and into the water on the other side, followed by the man and the other woman. They wanted help, that was all. Instinctively, Jim offered his hand and led them across the river. He was actually touching an Auca. He had spoken Auca phrases and been understood.

The three Indians were curious and friendly. Jim did not know how these three had come to the river. Were they official representatives of the tribe, or was the man simply an adventurous person who had insisted the two women come with him? Did their presence mean that a more "official" visit would happen soon? Many questions were unanswered as the team dealt with the excitement of the moment. The man and the girl were soon dubbed George and Delilah.

The hand-gesture communication continued all afternoon. The missionaries entertained the Auca visitors with all the gifts and trinkets they had brought with them precisely for this purpose. In between these interactions, the missionaries discussed the significance of this meeting. Did it mean that a larger group of Aucas was nearby? Or would a representative group come to Palm Beach and invite the missionaries to visit the Auca settlement? This is really what they wanted. Now they had to wait to see if it would happen.

As darkness approached, Nate and Pete had to leave. They could carry with them to Arajuno, and by radio to Shell Mera as well, the news of the first contact with Aucas.

George, Delilah, and the other woman remained on the beach, perhaps intending to spend the night. Eventually, Delilah wandered back into the trees, and George followed her. The older woman stayed by the fire most of the night, but she was gone in the morning.

Saturday, January 7, dawned with anticipation. Anxious to see what the new day would bring, Nate and Pete flew back in. The wait continued. Would George and the women come back? Would others come?

Disappointed that no Aucas had appeared on the beach that morning, Jim Elliot grew impatient. At one point, he threatened to cross the river and go find the Aucas himself. He soon regained his level head and did not carry out this intention, but he did go scouting around the forest looking for fresh footprints. He found none.

Equally restless, Pete and Nate decided to take a look from the air. They flew over the main settlement, and to their dismay, the Aucas seemed frightened. This was confusing; for weeks only friendly exchanges had occurred, with no sign that the Aucas were fearful of the plane or the people in it. But now the women and children ran to hide. For reassurance, Nate threw down a blanket and a pair of shorts.

On the second pass over the settlement, George appeared, and by the third pass, the fear seemed to have subsided. But what had caused it in the first place? And what was keeping the Aucas from coming to Palm Beach? The missionaries had no visitors that day.

On Sunday, January 8, Nate flew over the Auca settlement and saw only women and children. Where were the men? Were they finally on their way to Palm Beach? Then a few minutes later, Nate spotted the men. The whole group was following a route that would take them to Palm Beach very soon. Nate landed on the beach, calling out, "This is it, guys!" Then he got on the radio to his wife, Marj, in Shell Mera and let her know the news. It was twelve-thirty. They agreed to speak again at four-thirty, after the meeting with the Aucas.

Promptly at four-thirty, Marj was at the radio waiting for contact from her husband. Olive Fleming, who had been ill and was recuperating at Shell Mera, was with her. But the call did not come. Marj knew Nate was a stickler for frequent, regular communication. It was one of his cardinal rules, and Nate had never broken it. He had always let Marj know where he was and what his circumstances were. With two radios on the beach, equipment failure was no better an explanation than forgetfulness. Silence could not be good news under any explanation that Marj could imagine. Soon it was too dark to expect that Nate and Pete could fly back that night.

The long night passed. In the morning Marj Saint and Olive Fleming came face to face with the reality they had feared during the dark hours of the night.

With the breaking light, Johnny Keenan, the other MAF pilot, took a plane up and flew over the Curaray River to scout for the missing men. Within a few minutes, he radioed to Marj that he had found Nate's plane, stripped of all its fabric; there was no sign of the men, but the damage to the plane was clearly reason for alarm.

Within minutes of this report, word went out literally around the world of the five men missing in hostile Auca territory. Marj called the other wives. Barbara Youderian and Marilou McCully came in from Arajuno. Elisabeth Elliot arrived from Shandia, along with Rachel Saint, Nate's sister. Nearly everyone was hopeful that some of the team would survive whatever had happened to them. In fact, Marilou left a note on her door at Arajuno and returned there after only a day in Shell Mera. Logically, the men would come to Arajuno first, and she wanted to be home when they arrived.[2]

On the third day that the men were missing, Johnny Keenan spotted a body floating in the river. From the air it was hard to tell who it was. But it meant that at least one of the men had not survived.

On the fourth day, the Air Force Rescue operation joined the search that a network of missionaries and Quichuas had been conducting. Someone sent for Marilou McCully to be brought back to Shell Mera. The wives braced themselves for the news the searchers brought. Four bodies had been spotted from the air, and the Quichuas on the ground had found the fifth. There were no survivors. And no information on what had happened. And no way to find out what had provoked the attack when every sign was that the Aucas were responding to the missionaries' friendship. The Aucas themselves had retreated into the jungle, once again beyond reach.

TWENTY

Elisabeth Elliot was a missionary. Her commitment to reaching the Aucas had not been decorative, simply to complement her husband's passion for pioneer missionary work. She acted under her own calling, as did the other wives.

With their husbands gone, each of the women had to decide whether they would remain in Ecuador or return to the States. Marilou McCully decided to return to the States for the birth of her third child, but she later returned to Quito to set up a home for missionary children who attended school in the city. Olive Fleming helped her set up the school and then returned to the States. Barbara Youderian returned to work among the Jívaros. Marj Saint took up a new post in Quito. Elisabeth Elliot returned to Shandia, where she worked with Rachel Saint.

Rachel was studying the Auca language with Dayuma, the young woman who had helped Jim Elliot learn key phrases of friendship. Shortly after the killings at Palm Beach, Rachel Saint showed Dayuma photographs of "George" and "Delilah" and the other woman.

Dayuma excitedly recognized the other woman as her own aunt and Delilah as her cousin. Dayuma had left the Aucas because of a brutal family feud and had never been sure whether any of her family had survived. Knowing that her aunt was alive gave her hope that others in her family had also survived. This motivated Dayuma to consider returning to the Aucas, and thus she was the bridge that allowed white people further contact.

Later, when relations between missionaries and the Aucas were once again friendly because of the bridge Dayuma provided, Rachel Saint and Elisabeth Elliot actually moved to an Auca settlement for more intensive language study and to try to present the gospel to the Aucas.

Dayuma was a great help, not only because she aided in continuing language work, but also because she herself had become a Christian. While Elisabeth lived among the tribe, she collected information about that day on the beach, trying to find out just what had happened to Jim and the others—and why.

Elisabeth Elliot left the Auca work after a few years and returned to live in the States. Rachel Saint stayed on for many years, nurturing the church that emerged among the Aucas. But even as she lived among them for decades, Rachel did not persist in questions about the deaths of her brother and the other men. That was not her purpose, and too many questions perhaps could have endangered the work she was doing. Continued questioning might even have put her own life at risk. Of necessity, many questions remained unanswered for many years.

Thirty-three years after the Palm Beach deaths, Olive Fleming returned to the scene. She had remarried about two years after Pete's death and now traveled to Ecuador with her husband and the youngest of their three children.

In the years in between, she had known of Rachel and Elisabeth's work, the conversion of the Aucas to Christianity, and that they were now known as the Waorani. This was their own name for themselves, whereas "Auca" had been a Quichua word referring to savagery.

Rachel Saint and a Wycliffe missionary named Catherine Peeke had reduced the Waorani language to a written form and translated portions of the Bible into Waorani. Unlike thirty-three years earlier, it was now perfectly safe for Olive and her family to visit Palm Beach.

Except for one flight over the watery grave with the other widows, Olive had never seen Palm Beach. She now saw where the men had built their shelter, though the beach itself had changed over the decades. The pictures that Olive had seen of smooth sand and clear water did not resemble the scene before her now. Even the tree that had once held the treehouse thirty-five feet off the ground had been wrenched out of the ground by high water.

One of the Waorani women, Dawa, began speaking, intuitively answering the questions Olive was hesitant to ask. Dawa had witnessed the killings all those years ago and had been amazed that the missionaries had not used their guns to defend themselves.

In their planning, the men had agreed that they would not fire at the Waorani to preserve their own lives, and when the moment had come, they had stood by the decision they had made. They had fired into the air, trying to frighten their attackers, but they'd let the Waorani kill them. This was not new information to Rachel Saint, but it helped answer some questions for Olive.

However, Dawa had more information. Now even Rachel Saint listened intently to a story she had never heard before. Dawa recounted how, on the day that "George" and the others had visited the beach, one of the men had taken something out of his pocket to show to them.

In 1956 the Waoranis did not wear clothing and did not understand the concept of pockets. It seemed to them that the man was taking something out of his body. What he took out was a photograph of Dayuma. The men had carried the photo in hope that the Aucas would recognize Dayuma, and that she would be a bridge of friendship. Perhaps they wanted to explain that she was still alive.

But just as they did not understand pockets, the Waoranis did not understand photography. What had the strangers done to Dayuma to make her flat and small? How could Dayuma come out of the man's body? How had she gotten in there? The obvious conclusion was that the man had eaten Dayuma. When the three visitors told this story to the rest of the tribe, fear spread that the missionaries were cannibals who intended to eat the Waoranis. They would have to be killed.[1]

And so they were.

Rachel Saint was as surprised by this information as Olive Fleming Liefeld was. She had lived among these people for a long time. Why had she not heard this story before?

Dawa's account gave a long-awaited explanation for what had prompted the hostile behavior by the Waoranis in an otherwise friendly atmosphere. In all their careful strategizing and planning, the men had made one small error. In all of their guessing about how the Aucas might respond to various overtures of friendship, they had miscalculated how they would respond to something they did not understand. An innocent, ordinary photograph had cost them their lives.

But this was not the end of Dawa's story. Kimo, a Waorani Christian leader, was with the killers on the beach that day and joined Dawa's account of what happened in 1956. More surprises were in store, even for Rachel Saint.

When the men were dead and their bodies lying on the beach, the Waoranis heard singing. Dawa was in the woods and others on the beach when they looked up over the tops of the trees and saw a large group of people singing. They described it by saying it looked like "a hundred flashlights."

At the time, they had had no idea they were seeing angels, and they were understandably frightened by the vision. Had their actions brought on this strange vision? they wondered. Only years later, when they had heard and understood the gospel, did the Waoranis realize what they had seen.

Dawa later told Rachel that it was that vision on the beach that had first persuaded her to believe in God, and Dawa had become the first Christian in the tribe five years later.[2]

Pete, Ed, Roger, Nate, and Jim had given their lives trying to reach the Waoranis. At the time, it might have seemed that they failed. But thirty-three years later, a savage tribe was living peaceably with its neighbors and teaching the Christian faith. According to Dawa and Kimo, it had all begun with a vision of "a hundred flashlights."

Three years after Olive Fleming Liefeld's return to Palm Beach and thirty-six years after the killings, the Waorani Indians celebrated having the entire New Testament in their own language. The Waorani president said at the ceremony: "We no longer want to live as the old ones who killed each other and outsiders. We want to live by what God says. Ever since I was a small boy in this community, I have heard that we were going to get this book; now we have it!"[3]

AFTERWORD

Was it God's will for five missionaries to die trying to reach the Aucas—or Waoranis—with the gospel? Did they die because they were obedient?

This is the first question to spring to the minds of many people who hear the story of Jim Elliot and the other members of the Operation Auca team. They were young men who could have spent another forty years on the mission field. Imagine the impact that their five lives could have had in Ecuador during those decades, among the expansive Quichuas and other unevange-lized—but peaceful—tribes. Thousands might have been converted and dozens of churches born. But the team did not choose the safe option. With hearts full of conviction that what they were doing was what God wanted them to do, they took the more difficult road.

Surely God is powerful enough that He could have controlled the Aucas' frightened impulses long enough for them to hear the good news of the gospel.

So why didn't He?

The fact that Elisabeth Elliot, Rachel Saint, and Catherine Peeke eventually lived among the tribe and reached them with Christianity is some consolation. The dream of the five young men did not die with them. What they started out to do was finally done—interestingly—by women, rather than the single male missionaries Jim Elliot had thought were the only suitable candidates for pioneer missionary work.

Olive Fleming Liefeld's 1989 discovery of the story of "a hundred flashlights" also brings some consolation. It would appear that the event of the deaths of the men communicated something of the power and greatness of God long before words could tell the story. A question some have raised, though, is why this story did not come out sooner, since several missionaries had lived with the tribe for years. How precise was the account after thirty years? More questions with no answers.

The deaths were not in vain. But were they necessary? This is not such an easy question. Did Jim and the others rush into something they were not fully ready for? Some have said so. Perhaps they themselves were ready spiritually, but a more cautious effort would have had a different result. What if they had waited until after the rainy season that year and spent those months gathering more information and learning more language?

Jim had longed to go to the Aucas for years. They represented truly pioneer, genuinely primitive missionary work. This was the pinnacle of serving God, and Jim had never settled for anything less than the best. Was Jim perhaps too eager to reach the Aucas quickly?

Did the combination of Jim's purposefulness and Nate Saint's availability with a plane push them too fast?

Jim had been heavily influential in the lives of Pete Fleming and Ed McCully. Without his urging, would they have even been in Ecuador at all?

Of course, we can never know the answer to these questions, nor should we need to.

We may not be able to say definitively that the deaths were God's will or that they could have been avoided. But at the very least we can be sure that God's power brought good out of a tragic event in a dramatic way.

The deaths were widely covered in the news media of the day, including the prestigious *Life* magazine. Christians all over North America sat up and took note of the seriousness of the call of God on their lives.

Jim Elliot's journals were published when they might not otherwise have been. Thousands of readers have been influenced by his singularity of purpose in living a life wholly given over to God. With all his humanity and weaknesses, this remained his goal.

David Howard went on to a missionary career in Latin America and later was the international president of World Evangelical Fellowship. In his world-wide travels over twenty years, he frequently found people who told him that they were serving the Lord because of the impact of the life and death of Jim Elliot. When people learn of David's relationship to Elisabeth and Jim, they often share how Jim's journals or Elisabeth's writings about Jim's life were part of the way they were called into mission work.

Possibly in his death, Jim Elliot did more to spur interest in missions than if he had spent a long life speaking to student groups and churches. He gave God all he had to give and by his death inspired many others to do the same.

NOTES

CHAPTER 1
  1. Elisabeth Elliot, *Shadow of the Almighty: The Life and Testament of Jim Elliot* (Grand Rapids: Zondervan, 1970), 31.

CHAPTER 2
  1. Elisabeth Elliot, *Shadow of the Almighty: The Life and Testament of Jim Elliot* (Grand Rapids: Zondervan, 1970), 39.
  2. Ibid., 40.
  3. Ibid., 43.
  4. Ibid., 45.

CHAPTER 3
  1. Jim Elliot, *The Journals of Jim Elliot*, Elisabeth Elliot, ed. (Old Tappan, N.J.: Fleming H. Revell, 1978), 18.
  2. Ibid., 49.
  3. Ibid., 50.
  4. Elisabeth Elliot, *Passion and Purity: Learning to Bring Your Love Life Under Control* (Grand Rapids: Fleming H. Revell, 1984), 34.
  5. Ibid., 34–35.
  6. Ibid., 60.
  7. Jim Elliot, *The Journals of Jim Elliot*, Elisabeth Elliot, ed. (Old Tappan, N.J.: Revell, 1978), 65.
  8. Ibid.

CHAPTER 4

1. Jim Elliot, *The Journals of Jim Elliot*, Elisabeth Elliot, ed. (Old Tappan, N.J.: Revell, 1978), 80.
2. Ibid., 88.
3. Ibid., 88.
4. Elisabeth Elliot, *Shadow of the Almighty: The Life and Testament of Jim Elliot* (Grand Rapids: Zondervan 1970), 67.
5. Jim Elliot, *The Journals of Jim Elliot*, Elisabeth Elliot, ed. (Old Tappan, N.J.: Revell, 1978), 90.
6. Elisabeth Elliot, *Passion and Purity: Learning to Bring Your Love Life Under Control* (Grand Rapids: Fleming H. Revell, 1984), 120.
7. Jim Elliot, *The Journals of Jim Elliot*, Elisabeth Elliot, ed. (Old Tappan, N.J.: Revell, 1978), 101.
8. Elisabeth Elliot, *Shadow of the Almighty: The Life and Testament of Jim Elliot* (Grand Rapids: Zondervan, 1970), 75.
9. Jim Elliot, *The Journals of Jim Elliot*, Elisabeth Elliot, ed. (Old Tappan, N.J.: Revell, 1978), 107.
10. Elisabeth Elliot, *Shadow of the Almighty: The Life and Testament of Jim Elliot* (Grand Rapids: Zondervan, 1970), 87.
11. Ibid., 88.
12. Ibid., 89.
13. Jim Elliot, *The Journals of Jim Elliot*, Elisabeth Elliot, ed. (Old Tappan, N.J.: Revell, 1978), 110.
14. Ibid., 114.

CHAPTER 5

1. Jim Elliot, *The Journals of Jim Elliot*, Elisabeth Elliot, ed. (Old Tappan, N.J.: Revell, 1978), 119.
2. Elisabeth Elliot, *Shadow of the Almighty: The Life*

and Testament of Jim Elliot (Grand Rapids: Zondervan, 1970), 99.

CHAPTER 6

1. Jim Elliot, *The Journals of Jim Elliot,* Elisabeth Elliot, ed. (Old Tappan, N.J.: Revell, 1978), 140–141.
2. Elisabeth Elliot, *Shadow of the Almighty: The Life and Testament of Jim Elliot* (Grand Rapids: Zondervan, 1970), 104.
3. Jim Elliot, *The Journals of Jim Elliot, Elisabeth Elliot,* ed. (Old Tappan, N.J.: Revell, 1978), 142.
4. Elisabeth Elliot, *Passion and Purity: Learning to Bring Your Love Life Under Control* (Grand Rapids: Fleming H. Revell, 1984), 140.
5. Jim Elliot, *The Journals of Jim Elliot, Elisabeth Elliot,* ed. (Old Tappan, N.J.: Revell, 1978), 154.
6. Ibid., 200–201.

CHAPTER 7

1. Jim Elliot, *The Journals of Jim Elliot,* Elisabeth Elliot, ed. (Old Tappan, N.J.: Revell, 1978), 261.
2. Ibid., 263.
3. Elisabeth Elliot, *Shadow of the Almighty: The Life and Testament of Jim Elliot* (Grand Rapids: Zondervan, 1970), 132.
4. Jim Elliot, *The Journals of Jim Elliot,* Elisabeth Elliot, ed. (Old Tappan, N.J.: Revell, 1978), 269.
5. Ibid., 283.

CHAPTER 8

1. Jim Elliot, *The Journals of Jim Elliot,* Elisabeth Elliot, ed. (Old Tappan, N.J.: Revell, 1978), 318.

2. Ibid., 335.
3. Elisabeth Elliot, *Shadow of the Almighty: The Life and Testament of Jim Elliot* (Grand Rapids: Zondervan, 1970), 149.
4. Olive Fleming Liefeld, *Unfolding Destinies* (Grand Rapids: Zondervan, 1990), 44ff.
5. Jim Elliot, *The Journals of Jim Elliot*, Elisabeth Elliot, ed. (Old Tappan, N.J.: Revell, 1978, 342.
6. Ibid., 346.
7. Ibid., 346.
8. Ibid., 347.
9. Ibid., 349.
10. Ibid., 349.
11. Ibid., 350.
12. Elisabeth Elliot, *Passion and Purity: Learning to Bring Your Love Life Under Control* (Grand Rapids: Fleming H. Revell, 1984), 158.

CHAPTER 9
1. Elisabeth Elliot, *Shadow of the Almighty: The Life and Testament of Jim Elliot* (Grand Rapids: Zondervan, 1970), 169.
2. Ibid., 170–171.
3. Jim Elliot, *The Journals of Jim Elliot*, Elisabeth Elliot, ed. (Old Tappan, N.J.: Revell, 1978), 370.
4. Ibid., 371.
5. Ibid., 375.
6. Ibid., 377.
7. Ibid., 379.
8. Elisabeth Elliot, *Shadow of the Almighty: The Life and Testament of Jim Elliot* (Grand Rapids: Zondervan, 1970), 178.

CHAPTER 10
1. Jim Elliot, *The Journals of Jim Elliot*, Elisabeth Elliot, ed. (Old Tappan, N.J.: Revell, 1978), 397.
2. Elisabeth Elliot, *Shadow of the Almighty: The Life and Testament of Jim Elliot* (Grand Rapids: Zondervan, 1970), 186.
3. Ibid., 189.

CHAPTER 11
1. Elisabeth Elliot, *Shadow of the Almighty: The Life and Testament of Jim Elliot* (Grand Rapids: Zondervan, 1970), 190.
2. Ibid., 191–193.
3. Ibid., 194–195.
4. Ibid., 194.
5. Elisabeth Elliot, *Through Gates of Splendor* (New York: Harper & Brothers, 1957), 45.

CHAPTER 12
1. Jim Elliot, *The Journals of Jim Elliot*, Elisabeth Elliot, ed. (Old Tappan, N.J.: Revell, 1978), 436–437.
2. Ibid., 437.

CHAPTER 13
1. Elisabeth Elliot, *Shadow of the Almighty: The Life and Testament of Jim Elliot* (Grand Rapids: Zondervan, 1970), 206.

CHAPTER 14
1. Elisabeth Elliot, *Shadow of the Almighty: The Life*

and Testament of Jim Elliot (Grand Rapids: Zondervan, 1970), 223–4.

CHAPTER 15
1. Olive Fleming Liefeld, *Unfolding Destinies* (Grand Rapids: Zondervan, 1990), 187.
2. Elisabeth Elliot, *Through Gates of Splendor* (New York: Harper & Brothers, 1957), 59–60.

CHAPTER 16
1. Elisabeth Elliot, *Through Gates of Splendor* (New York: Harper & Brothers, 1957), 97.
2. Ibid., 99–100.
3. Ibid., 102.
4. Ibid., 130.
5. Ibid., 103.
6. Ibid., 104.

CHAPTER 17
1. Elisabeth Elliot, *Through Gates of Splendor* (New York: Harper & Brothers, 1957), 137ff.
2. Jim Elliot, *The Journals of Jim Elliot*, Elisabeth Elliot, ed. (Old Tappan, N.J.: Revell, 1978), 470–471.
3. Elisabeth Elliot, *Through Gates of Splendor* (New York: Harper & Brothers, 1957), 145.
4. Jim Elliot, *The Journals of Jim Elliot*, Elisabeth Elliot, ed. (Old Tappan, N.J.: Revell, 1978), 475.
5. Elisabeth Elliot, *Shadow of the Almighty: The Life and Testament of Jim Elliot* (Grand Rapids: Zondervan, 1970), 236.
6. Olive Fleming Liefeld, *Unfolding Destinies* (Grand Rapids: Zondervan, 1990), 191.

CHAPTER 18

1. Elisabeth Elliot, *Through Gates of Splendor* (New York: Harper & Brothers, 1957), 159.
2. Ibid., 160.
3. Olive Fleming Liefeld, *Unfolding Destinies* (Grand Rapids: Zondervan, 1990), 195–197.
4. Ibid., 198.
5. Elisabeth Elliot, *Through Gates of Splendor* (New York: Harper & Brothers, 1957), 177.
6. Elisabeth Elliot, *Shadow of the Almighty: The Life and Testament of Jim Elliot* (Grand Rapids: Zondervan, 1970), 244.

CHAPTER 19

1. Elisabeth Elliot, *Through Gates of Splendor* (New York: Harper & Brothers, 1957), 180–182.
2. Ibid., 197.

CHAPTER 20

1. Olive Fleming Liefeld, *Unfolding Destinies* (Grand Rapids: Zondervan, 1990), 235.
2. Ibid., 237.
3. "Dedication of Auca New Testament," *Catalyst*, Vol. 6, No. 2–3 (1995), 8–9.

HEROES OF THE FAITH

This exciting biographical series explores the lives of famous Christian men and women throughout the ages. These books will inspire and encourage you to follow the example of these "Heroes of the Faith" who made Christ the center of their existence.

208 pages / Only $1.99 each!

Amy Carmichael
Billy Graham
Corrie ten Boom
David Livingstone
Fanny Crosby
Florence Nightingale
Frederick Douglass
Free Indeed
Into All the World
Jim Elliot
Martin Luther
Well with My Soul